Manual for the
TEACHER'S
REPORT FORM

and
1991 PROFILE

Thomas M. Achenbach
Department of Psychiatry
University of Vermont

NOTE: Windows software is available for the TRF and other instruments of the Achenbach System of Empirically Based Assessment (ASEBA).

All **ASEBA** materials can be ordered from:

ASEBA
1 South Prospect St.
Burlington, VT 05401-3456
Web: http://Checklist.uvm.edu   Fax: 802/656-2602

Proper bibliographic citation for this *Manual*:

Achenbach, T.M. (1991). *Manual for the Teacher's Report Form and 1991 Profile.* Burlington, VT: University of Vermont Department of Psychiatry.

Related Books

Achenbach, T.M. (1991). *Manual for the Child Behavior Checklist/4-18 and 1991 Profile.* Burlington, VT: University of Vermont Department of Psychiatry.

Achenbach, T.M. (1991). *Manual for the Youth Self-Report and 1991 Profile.* Burlington, VT: University of Vermont Department of Psychiatry.

Achenbach, T.M. (1993). *Empirically based taxonomy: How to use syndromes and profile types derived from the CBCL/4-18, TRF, and YSR.* Burlington, VT: University of Vermont Department of Psychiatry.

Achenbach, T.M. (1997). *Manual for the Young Adult Self-Report and Young Adult Behavior Checklist.* Burlington, VT: University of Vermont Department of Psychiatry.

Achenbach, T.M., & McConaughy, S.H. (1997). *Empirically based assessment of child and adolescent psychopathology: Practical applications.* (2nd ed.) Thousand Oaks, CA: Sage Publications.

Library of Congress #90-72108   ISBN 0-938565-10-9

Printed in the United States of America 12 11 10 9

USER QUALIFICATIONS

The Teacher's Report Form (TRF) is designed to be filled out by teachers who have known a pupil in a school setting for at least two months. Because the TRF is self-explanatory, no special qualifications are needed for administering it. When a teacher is asked to complete the TRF, however, it is helpful to explain that the aim is to obtain a description of the pupil's behavior as the teacher sees it. Because the TRF is designed for many kinds of pupils, some items may not seem applicable to a particular pupil. If teachers question the appropriateness of certain items, they should use the response categories provided but can elaborate by writing additional information if desired. On the problem items, for example, if a teacher does not know whether a particular kind of behavior occurs, it is appropriate to circle 0, meaning "Not true (as far as you know)," although the teacher may also wish to write in that there has been no chance to observe it. If a pupil is handicapped or in a special class, the teacher should base ratings on standards expected for typical (i.e., "normal") pupils of that pupil's age. This is necessary to provide an appropriate basis for comparison with the normative data on which standard scores are based.

To make proper use of data from the TRF, it is important to score the teacher's responses on the appropriate scoring profile and to compare the results with data from other sources, such as parents, other teachers who know the pupil, observers, interviews with the pupil, and standardized tests. The user must therefore have access to multiple sources of data and must be trained in the theory and methodology of standardized assessment, as well as in work with teachers and children. The training required will differ according to the specific application of the instruments, but graduate training of at least the Master's degree level is usually necessary. No amount of prior training, however, can substitute for professional maturity and a thorough knowledge of the procedures and cautions presented in this *Manual*.

All users should understand that our instruments are designed to provide standardized descriptions of behavior, rather than diagnostic inferences. No scores on the TRF scales should be automatically equated with any particular diagnosis or inferred disorder. Instead, the responsible professional will integrate teacher data with other types of data in the comprehensive evaluation of the child and family.

PREFACE

This *Manual* provides basic information needed for understanding and using the Teacher's Report Form (TRF) and its scoring profile. It also outlines the TRF's relations to other instruments we have developed, especially the Child Behavior Checklist for Ages 4-18 (CBCL/4-18) and the Youth Self-Report (YSR). The Reader's Guide following this Preface offers an overview of the contents to aid users in quickly locating the material they seek.

To aid users in moving between the TRF, CBCL/4-18, and YSR, the *Manuals* for the three instruments follow similar formats. In addition, the *Integrative Guide for the 1991 CBCL/4-18, YSR, and TRF Profiles* details relations among the profiles for the three instruments and the procedures for deriving syndromes that are common to all three.

The pre-1991 profiles for scoring the TRF, CBCL, and YSR were developed separately as data were accumulated for each one. The syndrome scales of each profile were designed to capture the patterns of problems specifically identified for each sex within particular age ranges on each instrument taken separately.

The pre-1991 syndrome scales functioned well for describing and assessing patterns that were empirically derived for specific sex/age groups as seen by a particular type of informant. The 1991 editions are designed to advance both the conceptual structure and the practical applications of empirically based assessment by focusing more precisely on the syndromes that are common to both sexes and different age ranges, according to teacher-, parent-, and self-reports.

The 1991 profiles for scoring data from all three sources include a common set of eight syndromes that are normed on the same national sample. However, to reflect important sex and age differences, the syndromes are normed separately for each sex within particular age ranges, according to reports by each type of informant. In addition, items found to be associated with a syndrome in ratings by a particular type of informant are retained for scoring by that type of informant. Some additional syndromes and competence scales are also specific to particular sex/age groups on the CBCL and YSR but not on the TRF.

Although this *Manual* was written by a single author, the first person plural "we" is used throughout. This reflects the author's feeling that the work is a joint product of many coworkers, especially the following: Neil Aguiar, Janet Arnold, Jill Brown, Bruce Compas, Craig Edelbrock,

Judy Ewell, Catherine Howell, Lynda Howell, David Jacobowitz, Stephanie McConaughy, Susan Oakes, Vicky Phares, Michael Sawyer, Catherine Stanger, Gavin Stewart, Frank Verhulst, and John Weisz. I deeply appreciate the contributions of all these people, plus the many others who have contributed through their own work and comments. I am most grateful for the Spencer Foundation's support of our recent research on teachers' reports. Much of the work reported here has also been supported by University Associates in Psychiatry, a nonprofit health services and research corporation of the University of Vermont Department of Psychiatry.

READER'S GUIDE

I. **Introductory Material Needed by Most Readers**

   A. Description of the TRF
      and Multiaxial Assessment .... **Chapter 1**
   B. Academic and Adaptive Scores .... **Chapter 2**
   C. Problem Scales Scored from the TRF .... **Chapter 3**
   D. Internalizing and Externalizing
      Groupings of Syndromes .... **Chapter 4**

II. **Statistical Data on Reliability and Validity**

   A. Reliability, Stability,
      and Inter-Teacher Agreement .... **Chapter 5**
   B. Validity .... **Chapter 6**
   C. Item Scores .... **Chapter 7**

III. **Relations Between the Pre-1991**
    and 1991 Scales .... **Chapter 8**

IV. **Applications of the TRF and Profile**

   A. Practical Applications .... **Chapter 9**
   B. Research Use .... **Chapter 10**

V. **Instruments Related to the TRF** .... **Chapter 11**

VI. **Answers to Commonly Asked Questions** .... **Chapter 12**

VII. **Instructions for Hand Scoring**
    the Profile .... **Appendix A**

VIII. **Mean Scale Scores for Matched Referred**
     and Nonreferred Samples .... **Appendix B**

IX. **Correlations Among Scales** .... **Appendix C**

CONTENTS

User Qualifications iii

Preface iv

Reader's Guide v

1. **The Teacher's Report Form** 1
   Multiaxial Empirically Based Assessment 2
   Academic and Adaptive Functioning Items of the TRF 4
   Problem Items of the TRF 4
   Administration of the TRF 11
   Summary 12

2. **Academic and Adaptive Functioning Scales** 14
   Norming the Academic and Adaptive Functioning Scales 14
   Assignment of Percentiles and T Scores 16
   Summary 20

3. **Syndrome and Total Problem Scales** 23
   Pre-1991 Syndromes 24
   Derivation of the 1991 Syndromes 25
      Principal Components Analyses 26
      Rotations of Principal Components 27
      Analysis of 89 Common Items 30
      Derivation of Core Syndromes 30
      Cross-Informant Syndromes 32
   Profiles for Scoring the 1991 Syndromes 34
   Assigning Normalized T Scores to Syndrome Scales 37
      Lowest T Scores 38
      Highest T Scores 39
   Assigning Normalized T Scores to Total Problem Scores 40
   Normal, Borderline, and Clinical Ranges 45
      Syndrome Scales 45
      Total Problem Score 46
   Summary 47

4. **Internalizing and Externalizing Groupings of Syndromes** ... 49
   1991 Internalizing and Externalizing Groupings 50
   Assignment of Internalizing and Externalizing T Scores 52
   Relations between Internalizing and Externalizing Scores 53
      Distinguishing Between Internalizing and Externalizing Patterns . 54
   Summary 55

5. **Reliability, Stability, and Inter-Teacher Agreement** 57
   Test-Retest Reliability of Scores 58

Two- and Four-Month Stability of Problem Scores 59
Inter-Teacher Agreement 60
   Odds Ratios for Scores in the Normal versus Clinical Range ... 61
   Correlations Between Teachers and Teacher Aides 63
Summary 65

6. Validity 66
   Content Validity 66
   Construct Validity 68
   Criterion-Related Validity 71
      Referral Status Differences Between Scale Scores 73
      Demographic Differences Between Scale Scores 75
   Classification of Pupils According to Clinical Cutpoints 79
      Odds Ratios 80
      Combined Academic, Adaptive, and Problem Scores 81
      Discriminant Analyses 83
   Probability of Particular Scores Being from the
   Referred Versus Nonreferred Samples 86
   Summary 88

7. Item Scores 90
   Academic and Adaptive Scores 90
      Demographic Differences in Academic and Adaptive Scores 92
   Problem Item Scores 94
      Referral Status Differences in Problem Scores 95
      Demographic Differences in Problem Scores 102
   Summary 123

8. Relations Between Pre-1991 and 1991 TRF Scales 125
   Construction of Scales 126
      Syndrome Scales 126
      Internalizing and Externalizing 128
      Total Problem Score 129
   Statistical Relations between Pre-1991 and 1991 Scales 129
   Summary 131

9. Practical Applications of the TRF and Profile 132
   School-Based Service Applications 134
      Teachers' Concerns and Referrals 134
      Comparison of Pupils' Functioning in Different Classes 137
      Evaluation of Parents' Concerns 140
      Relations to Cognitive Functioning 141
      Relations to Medical Factors 143
      Relations to Specific Environmental Factors 144
   Comprehensive Evaluation for Special Services 146

Case Example 147
Re-Evaluation of Pupils 153
Applications in Mental Health Contexts 154
    Referrals.. 154
    Use by Mental Health Services 154
Needs Assessment and Program Accountability 155
    Needs Assessment 155
    Program Accountability 156
Use of the Profile Outside Its Normative Age Range 157
Training of School Personnel 158
    Teachers....................................... 158
    Special Educators 158
    School Psychologists 159
Summary 160

10. **Research Use of the TRF and Profile** 163
Use of Raw Scores Versus *T* Scores in Research with the TRF 165
    Statistical Analysis of Scale Scores 167
Research Spanning Multiple Sex/Age Groups 168
Outcome Research 172
Services Research 174
    Experimental Intervention Studies 174
    Operations Research 175
Research on Child Abuse 176
Research on Medical Conditions 176
Cross-Cultural Research 177
Summary 179

11. **Assessment Materials Related to the TRF** 180
Summary 183

12. **Answers to Commonly Asked Questions** 184
Questions about the TRF 184
Scoring the TRF 189
1991 TRF Profile 191

References 196
Appendix
A. Instructions for Handscoring the TRF 201
B. Scale scores for Referred and Nonreferred Samples 204
C. Correlations Among *T* Scores 208
Index 212

Chapter 1
The Teacher's Report Form

This is a revision of the *Manual for the Teacher's Report Form and Teacher Version of the Child Behavior Profile* (Achenbach & Edelbrock, 1986). The current revision is necessitated by changes in the 1991 scoring profile, new national norms through age 18, and new provisions for coordinating data from teacher-, parent-, and self-reports.

Some small changes were made in the 1988 and 1991 editions of the Teacher's Report Form (TRF), but these do not affect scoring. The main change in item wording on the 1991 TRF is in problem Item *42*, which has been changed to *Would rather be alone than with others*, from the pre-1991 version *Likes to be alone*. All pre-1991 editions of the TRF can be scored on the 1991 profile. Conversely, the 1991 edition of the TRF can be scored on the earlier versions of the profile, except that the pre-1991 profiles do not include norms for ages 17 and 18. Continuity can thus be maintained in scoring data obtained at any time with any edition of the TRF.

To aid readers who are unfamiliar with the TRF, as well as those who are familiar with it, this *Manual* first presents the multiaxial assessment model on which the TRF is based. Thereafter, the TRF itself is described. Chapter 2 presents the scales for scoring the academic performance and adaptive functioning items on the 1991 profile, while Chapter 3 presents the scales for scoring the problem items. Internalizing and Externalizing groupings of syndrome scales are presented in Chapter 4. Chapter 5 deals with reliability, stability, and inter-teacher agreement data for scores obtained from the TRF. Chapter 6 provides evidence for validity and the basis for cutpoints that distinguish between the normal, borderline, and clinical ranges.

Statistical and graphic comparisons of item scores obtained by referred and nonreferred pupils are presented in Chapter 7. Chapter 8 presents relations between the 1991 profile and the preceding edition. Applications in practical and research contexts are presented in Chapters 9 and 10, respectively. Chapter 11 describes relations between the TRF and the closely related Child Behavior Checklist for Ages 4-18 (CBCL/4-18) and Youth Self-Report (YSR). Chapter 12 provides answers to commonly asked questions. Instructions for hand scoring the 1991 TRF profile can be found in Appendix A, while psychometric data on the scale scores are displayed in Appendix B and C.

MULTIAXIAL EMPIRICALLY BASED ASSESSMENT

For the assessment of children attending school, teachers' reports of adaptive functioning and problems are extremely important for the following reasons:

1. School is a central developmental arena in which problems arise that may not be evident elsewhere.

2. School-based social and academic skills are important for successful adaptive development in our society.

3. Teachers are often the second most important adults in children's lives, ranking only behind parents.

4. By virtue of training, experience, and opportunities for observing children in groups, teachers can report aspects of children's functioning not evident to parents.

5. Teachers' reports are not apt to be affected by family dynamics, although they are affected by the interpersonal dynamics of the school setting.

6. Teachers are often involved in the referral and assessment of children for special services, both within the school and elsewhere.

The TRF is designed to obtain teachers' reports of their pupils' adaptive functioning and problems in a standardized format. It is modeled on the CBCL/4-18, which was developed to obtain parents' reports of their children's competencies and problems (Achenbach, 1991b). Although the TRF is designed primarily for teachers, it can also be completed by other school personnel who have similar knowledge of pupils' functioning, such as guidance counselors, administrators, and special educators.

The TRF provides an efficient and economical means for comparing a particular child's school functioning, as perceived by a particular teacher, with the functioning of normative samples of peers, as perceived by their teachers. It can also be used to compare the same child's functioning as depicted in reports by different teachers and other school personnel, such as guidance counselors. However, even for school-based assessment, additional sources of data are needed to provide a comprehensive picture of the child's functioning. Direct assessment of children via classroom observations, clinical interviews, and structured self-reports provide additional perspectives for which we have developed empirically based scoring systems whose findings can be compared with those obtained with the TRF. School-based assessment should also employ standardized tests of ability, achievement, perceptual-motor functioning, and speech-language skills. Because parents are typically involved in the assessment of their children and can provide important data not available to school personnel, their reports contribute an important component of assessment.

Medical diagnostic procedures are also important for the comprehensive assessment of most children.

To summarize the major components of assessment that are relevant to most children attending school, Table 1-1 presents examples of assessment procedures grouped according to five axes. It is not always feasible to employ assessment procedures from all five axes. However, as detailed elsewhere (Achenbach, 1991a), the value of any one assessment procedure, such as the TRF can be greatly enhanced by meshing it with other types of procedures. Procedures beside the kinds listed in Table 1-1 may also be helpful under certain conditions. Peer judgments, for example, may add another important perspective if appropriate parental permissions can be obtained for all the participating peers and if possible negative effects on the target children can be avoided.

ACADEMIC AND ADAPTIVE FUNCTIONING ITEMS OF THE TRF

As shown in Figure 1-1, page 1 of the TRF requests relevant background information (Items I-VI) and ratings of academic performance (Item VII). Page 2 requests ratings of four aspects of adaptive functioning (Item VIII): *1. How hard is he/she working? 2. How appropriately is he/she behaving? 3. How much is he/she learning? 4. How happy is he/she?* The ratings of academic performance and adaptive functioning are scored on the adaptive functioning portion of the TRF profile, as described in Chapter 2. The remaining items on page 2 request information that is useful for assessing children but that is too variable to be scored on the profile.

PROBLEM ITEMS OF THE TRF

As shown in Figure 1-2, pages 3 and 4 of the TRF list problem items to which teachers respond by circling *0* if the item is *not true* of the child (as far as the respondent knows);

Table 1-1
Examples of Multiaxial Assessment Procedures

Approx. Age Range	Axis I Parent Reports	Axis II Teacher Reports	Axis III Cognitive Assessment	Axis IV Physical Assessment	Axis V Direct Assessment of Child
5-11	CBCL/4-18 History Parent interview	TRF School records Teacher interview	Ability tests Achievement tests Perceptual-motor tests Language tests	Height, Weight Medical exam Neurological exam	DOF[a] SCIC[b]
12-18	CBCL/4-18 History Parent interview	TRF School records Teacher interview	Ability tests Achievement tests Perceptual-motor tests	Height, Weight Medical exam Neurological exam	DOF[a] YSR Clinical interview Self-Concept measures Personality tests

[a]DOF = Direct Observation Form (see McConaughy & Achenbach, 1988)
[b]SCIC = Semistructured Clinical Interview for Children (see McConaughy & Achenbach, 1990)

TEACHER'S REPORT FORM

	For office use only ID #

Your answers will be used to compare the pupil with other pupils whose teachers have completed similar forms. The information from this form will also be used for comparison with other information about this pupil. Please answer as well as you can, even if you lack full information. Scores on individual items will be combined to identify general patterns of behavior. Feel free to write additional comments beside each item and in the spaces provided on page 2.

PUPIL'S
NAME

PARENTS' USUAL TYPE OF WORK, even if not working now. *(Please be as specific as you can — for example, auto mechanic, high school teacher, homemaker, laborer, lathe operator, shoe salesman, army sergeant.)*

PUPIL'S SEX	PUPIL'S AGE	ETHNIC GROUP OR RACE
☐ Boy ☐ Girl		

FATHER'S
TYPE OF WORK: _____

MOTHER'S
TYPE OF WORK: _____

TODAY'S DATE	PUPIL'S BIRTHDATE (if known)
Mo.____ Date____ Yr.____	Mo.____ Date____ Yr.____

THIS FORM FILLED OUT BY:

☐ Teacher (name) _____

GRADE IN SCHOOL	NAME OF SCHOOL

☐ Counselor (name) _____

☐ Other (specify)
name: _____

I.   How long have you known this pupil? _____ months

II. How well do you know him/her?   1. ☐ Not Well   2. ☐ Moderately Well   3. ☐ Very Well

III. How much time does he/she spend in your class per week?

IV. What kind of class is it? (Please be specific, e.g., regular 5th grade, 7th grade math, etc.)

V.   Has he/she ever been referred for special class placement, services, or tutoring?
     ☐ Don't Know   0. ☐ No   1. ☐ Yes — what kind and when?

VI. Has he/she ever repeated a grade?
     ☐ Don't Know   0. ☐ No   1. ☐ Yes — grade and reason

VII. Current school performance — list academic subjects and check column that indicates pupil's performance:

Academic subject	1. Far below grade	2. Somewhat below grade	3. At grade level	4. Somewhat above grade	5. Far above grade
1. _____	☐	☐	☐	☐	☐
2. _____	☐	☐	☐	☐	☐
3. _____	☐	☐	☐	☐	☐
4. _____	☐	☐	☐	☐	☐
5. _____	☐	☐	☐	☐	☐
6. _____	☐	☐	☐	☐	☐

Figure 1-1. Page 1 of the TRF.

VIII. Compared to typical pupils of the same age:

	1. Much less	2. Somewhat less	3. Slightly less	4. About average	5. Slightly more	6. Somewhat more	7. Much more
1. How hard is he/she working?	□	□	□	□	□	□	□
2. How appropriately is he/she behaving?	□	□	□	□	□	□	□
3. How much is he/she learning?	□	□	□	□	□	□	□
4. How happy is he/she?	□	□	□	□	□	□	□

IX. Most recent achievement test scores (If available):

Name of test	Subject	Date	Percentile or grade level obtained

X. IQ, readiness, or aptitude tests (If available):

Name of test	Date	IQ or equivalent scores

Does this pupil have any illness, physical disability, or mental handicap?   □ No   □ Yes – please describe

What concerns you most about this pupil?

Please describe the best things about this pupil:

Please feel free to write any comments about this pupil's work, behavior, or potential, using extra pages if necessary.

Figure 1-1 (cont.). Page 2 of the TRF.

TEACHER'S REPORT FORM

Below is a list of items that describe pupils. For each item that describes the pupil **now or within the past 2 months**, please circle the **2** if the item is **very true** or **often true** of the pupil. Circle the **1** if the item is **somewhat** or **sometimes true** of the pupil. If the item is **not true** of the pupil, circle the **0**. Please answer all items as well as you can, even if some do not seem to apply to this pupil.

0 = Not True (as far as you know)   **1 = Somewhat or Sometimes True**   **2 = Very True or Often True**

0 1 2	1. Acts too young for his/her age	0 1 2	31. Fears he/she might think or do something bad
0 1 2	a 2. Hums or makes other odd noises in class	0 1 2	32. Feels he/she has to be perfect
0 1 2	3. Argues a lot	0 1 2	33. Feels or complains that no one loves him/her
0 1 2	a 4. Fails to finish things he/she starts	0 1 2	34. Feels others are out to get him/her
0 1 2	5. Behaves like opposite sex	0 1 2	35. Feels worthless or inferior
0 1 2	a 6. Defiant, talks back to staff	0 1 2	36. Gets hurt a lot, accident-prone
0 1 2	7. Bragging, boasting	0 1 2	37. Gets in many fights
0 1 2	8. Can't concentrate, can't pay attention for long	0 1 2	38. Gets teased a lot
0 1 2	9. Can't get his/her mind off certain thoughts; obsessions (describe): _____	0 1 2	39. Hangs around with others who get in trouble
		0 1 2	40. Hears sounds or voices that aren't there (describe):
		0 1 2	41. Impulsive or acts without thinking
0 1 2	10. Can't sit still, restless, or hyperactive	0 1 2	42. Would rather be alone than with others
0 1 2	11. Clings to adults or too dependent	0 1 2	43. Lying or cheating
		0 1 2	44. Bites fingernails
0 1 2	12. Complains of loneliness	0 1 2	45. Nervous, high-strung, or tense
0 1 2	13. Confused or seems to be in a fog	0 1 2	46. Nervous movements or twitching (describe):
0 1 2	14. Cries a lot		
0 1 2	a 15. Fidgets		
0 1 2	16. Cruelty, bullying, or meanness to others	0 1 2	a 47. Overconforms to rules
		0 1 2	48. Not liked by other pupils
0 1 2	17. Daydreams or gets lost in his/her thoughts		
0 1 2	18. Deliberately harms self or attempts suicide	0 1 2	a 49. Has difficulty learning
		0 1 2	50. Too fearful or anxious
0 1 2	19. Demands a lot of attention		
0 1 2	20. Destroys his/her own things	0 1 2	51. Feels dizzy
		0 1 2	52. Feels too guilty
0 1 2	21. Destroys property belonging to others		
0 1 2	a 22. Difficulty following directions	0 1 2	a 53. Talks out of turn
		0 1 2	54. Overtired
0 1 2	23. Disobedient at school		
0 1 2	a 24. Disturbs other pupils	0 1 2	55. Overweight
			56. Physical problems without known medical cause:
0 1 2	25. Doesn't get along with other pupils	0 1 2	a. Aches or pains (**not** headaches)
0 1 2	26. Doesn't seem to feel guilty after misbehaving	0 1 2	b. Headaches
		0 1 2	c. Nausea, feels sick
0 1 2	27. Easily jealous	0 1 2	d. Problems with eyes (describe):_____
0 1 2	28. Eats or drinks things that are not food—**don't** include sweets (describe):_____		
		0 1 2	e. Rashes or other skin problems
		0 1 2	f. Stomachaches or cramps
0 1 2	29. Fears certain animals, situations, or places other than school (describe): _____	0 1 2	g. Vomiting, throwing up
		0 1 2	h. Other (describe):_____
0 1 2	30. Fears going to school		

Figure 1-2. Problem Items 1-56h of the TRF. Superscript *a* indicates items that replace those on the CBCL/4-18.

TEACHER'S REPORT FORM   9

0 = Not True (as far as you know)   1 = Somewhat or Sometimes True   2 = Very True or Often True

0 1 2	57. Physically attacks people	0 1 2	84. Strange behavior (describe): _____
0 1 2	58. Picks nose, skin, or other parts of body (describe): _____	0 1 2	85. Strange ideas (describe): _____
0 1 2 ᵃ	59. Sleeps in class	0 1 2	86. Stubborn, sullen, or irritable
0 1 2 ᵃ	60. Apathetic or unmotivated	0 1 2	87. Sudden changes in mood or feelings
0 1 2	61. Poor school work	0 1 2	88. Sulks a lot
0 1 2	62. Poorly coordinated or clumsy	0 1 2	89. Suspicious
0 1 2	63. Prefers being with older children or youths	0 1 2	90. Swearing or obscene language
0 1 2	64. Prefers being with younger children	0 1 2	91. Talks about killing self
0 1 2	65. Refuses to talk	0 1 2 ᵃ	92. Underachieving, not working up to potential
0 1 2	66. Repeats certain acts over and over; compulsions (describe): _____	0 1 2	93. Talks too much
		0 1 2	94. Teases a lot
0 1 2 ᵃ	67. Disrupts class discipline	0 1 2	95. Temper tantrums or hot temper
0 1 2	68. Screams a lot	0 1 2	96. Seems preoccupied with sex
0 1 2	69. Secretive, keeps things to self	0 1 2	97. Threatens people
0 1 2	70. Sees things that aren't there (describe): _____	0 1 2 ᵃ	98. Tardy to school or class
		0 1 2	99. Too concerned with neatness or cleanliness
0 1 2	71. Self-conscious or easily embarrassed	0 1 2 ᵃ	100. Fails to carry out assigned tasks
0 1 2 ᵃ	72. Messy work	0 1 2	101. Truancy or unexplained absence
0 1 2 ᵃ	73. Behaves irresponsibly (describe): _____	0 1 2	102. Underactive, slow moving, or lacks energy
		0 1 2	103. Unhappy, sad, or depressed
0 1 2	74. Showing off or clowning	0 1 2	104. Unusually loud
0 1 2	75. Shy or timid	0 1 2	105. Uses alcohol or drugs for nonmedical purposes describe): _____
0 1 2 ᵃ	76. Explosive and unpredictable behavior	0 1 2 ᵃ	106. Overly anxious to please
0 1 2 ᵃ	77. Demands must be met immediately, easily frustrated	0 1 2 ᵃ	107. Dislikes school
0 1 2 ᵃ	78. Inattentive, easily distracted	0 1 2 ᵃ	108. Is afraid of making mistakes
0 1 2	79. Speech problem (describe): _____	0 1 2	109. Whining
		0 1 2 ᵃ	110. Unclean personal appearance
0 1 2	80. Stares blankly	0 1 2	111. Withdrawn, doesn't get involved with others
0 1 2 ᵃ	81. Feels hurt when criticized	0 1 2	112. Worries
0 1 2	82. Steals		113. Please write in any problems the pupil has that were not listed above:
0 1 2	83. Stores up things he/she doesn't need (describe): _____	0 1 2	_____
		0 1 2	_____
		0 1 2	_____

PAGE 4   *PLEASE BE SURE YOU HAVE ANSWERED ALL ITEMS*

Figure 1-2 (cont.) Problem items 57-113 of the TRF. Superscript *a* indicates items that replace those on the CBCL/4-18.

1 if the item is *somewhat or sometimes true*; and *2* if the item is *very true or often true.* The 0-1-2 response scale and problem items with no superscript in Figure 1-2 are counterparts of those on the CBCL (Achenbach, 1991b, presents the rationale for the problem list and response scale.) Items with superscript *a* in Figure 1-2 replace CBCL items that were inappropriate for teachers. Note that items are numbered 1-113, but that Item 56 includes physical problems *a* through *g.* The total number of problems listed is thus 118, plus space for other physical problems (Item 56h) and "any problems the pupil has that were not listed above" (Item 113). The similar items of the TRF and CBCL facilitate comparisons between the parent and teacher reports.

On several items, the teacher is asked to describe the behavior in question. This enables the user to avoid scoring problems not properly covered by that item or for which another item is more specific. Examples include *9. Can't get mind off certain thoughts, obsessions; 28. Eats or drinks things that are not food; 46. Nervous movements or twitching;* and *66. Repeats certain acts over and over, compulsions.* On other items, descriptions are requested to enable the user to determine the specific content of the problems the teacher is reporting. Examples include *29. Fears certain animals, situations, or places other than school; 40. Hears sounds or voices that aren't there; 56d. Problems with eyes; 58. Picks nose, skin, or other parts of body;* and *105. Uses alcohol or drugs for nonmedical purposes.* If teachers' descriptions of problems indicate that they have scored an item inappropriately or scored more than one item for the same problem, only the item that corresponds most precisely to the problem should be counted (see Appendix A for details of scoring).

Teachers are asked to base their ratings on the previous 2 months, in contrast to the 6-month period requested of parents on the CBCL. The shorter period was chosen to avoid restricting the use of teachers' ratings to the last part of the school year and to allow time for assessing change by repeating ratings within the same school year. The 6-month baseline period specified for parents' ratings is intended to pick up low frequency behaviors such as fire-setting, running away from home, and suicide attempts that are more likely to be known to parents than teachers. However, if a user wishes to compare parent and teacher ratings based on exactly the same periods, it is recommended that the instructions on page 3 of the parent CBCL be changed from 6 to 2 months to correspond to the 2-month baseline specified for the TRF.

ADMINISTRATION OF THE TRF

The TRF is designed to be self-administered by teachers. Most teachers can complete the structured items in about 10 minutes, although teachers who add extensive comments and scores from tests will need more time. Because teachers are requested to fill out many forms for which they may receive inadequate explanations, it is essential to explain the purpose of the TRF and to be available to answer the teacher's questions about it. If the TRF is used within a school system for psychological or special education evaluations, for example, the school psychologist or director of special education should show teachers the TRF in advance and explain that it is designed to obtain their important perspectives on pupils who are being evaluated. When a teacher is asked to complete a TRF, the school psychologist or special educator should communicate directly with the teacher about the importance of the teacher's views of the child and should be available to answer the teacher's questions. If a school system routinely uses the TRF in teacher-initiated referrals for evaluations and special services, teachers can be provided with copies to fill out on any child they wish to refer. This will help to make the TRF more familiar and to clarify its role in evaluating children.

The TRF profile is not intended to be used by the teacher who completes the TRF but by a school psychologist or other professional trained in psychological assessment. Like the YSR and CBCL, completed TRFs and scored profiles should not be accessible to unauthorized people.

If completion of the TRF is requested by a mental health professional or researcher from outside the school system, the TRF should be accompanied by a personal contact or letter to the teacher detailing the reason for the request and including a permission form signed by the child's parent or other responsible party. The requester should also be available to answer the teacher's questions.

As shown in Figure 1-1, the instructions on page 1 of the TRF explain that the teacher's answers will be used to compare the pupil with others whose teachers have completed similar forms. The instructions also explain that the information will be compared with other information about the pupil and that scores for individual items will be combined to identify general patterns of behavior. However, teachers may feel that they cannot answer some items accurately or that their answers to particular items may have grave consequences. It is therefore important to reassure them that any information they provide will be helpful and that they should feel free to write in additional comments and qualifiers wherever they wish.

SUMMARY

The present revision of the *Manual for the Teacher's Report Form* is necessitated by changes in the 1991 profile for scoring the TRF and new provisions for coordinating TRF data with CBCL and YSR data. Pre-1991 editions of the TRF can be scored on the 1991 TRF profile. Conversely, the 1991 edition of the TRF can be scored on pre-1991 TRF profiles.

The TRF is intended to serve as one component of *multiaxial empirically based assessment*. Other components include parent- and self-reports, standardized tests, physical assessment, observations, and interviews. The TRF requests teachers' ratings of performance in academic subjects, four adaptive characteristics, 118 specific problem items, and two open-ended problem items. The problem items are scored on a 3-step response scale like that used for the CBCL and YSR. Most of the problem items have counterparts on the CBCL and YSR, but teachers are asked to base ratings on the preceding 2 months, in contrast to the 6-month baseline used on the CBCL and YSR. The baseline periods can be changed if desired for specific applications.

Chapter 2
Academic and Adaptive Functioning Scales

As described in Chapter 1, pages 1 and 2 of the TRF provide items for obtaining ratings for academic performance and four adaptive characteristics. The teacher's ratings of performance in academic subjects are scored 1 to 5 for categories ranging from *Far below grade* to *Far above grade*, as shown for Item VII on page 1 of the TRF in Figure 1-1. The ratings for all academic subjects are averaged according to the instructions in Appendix A.

The teacher's ratings for the four adaptive characteristics are scored 1 to 7 for categories ranging from *Much less* to *Much more*, compared to typical pupils of the same age, as shown in Item VIII.1-4 on page 2 of the TRF in Figure 1-1. In addition, the scores for the four adaptive characteristics are summed to provide a global index of adaptive functioning, if all four items are rated.

NORMING THE ACADEMIC AND ADAPTIVE FUNCTIONING SCALES

Normative data for the TRF scales were drawn from a subset of subjects in a national sample assessed with the CBCL/4-18 in a home interview survey during the spring of 1989. Details of the procedure for obtaining data on the 7- to 18-year-olds in the sample have been provided by McConaughy, Stanger, and Achenbach (1991). These subjects were chosen to be representative of the 48 contiguous states with respect to socioeconomic status (SES), ethnicity, region, and urban-suburban-rural residence. Data for 5- and 6-year-olds were obtained under a separate contract by identifying households in the survey that were occupied by children in this age range, in addition to the initial 7- to 18-year-old subject. If there was more than one nonhandicapped 5- or 6-year-old in the household, a randomization procedure was used to select one for assessment.

For the 5- to 18-year-olds who were attending school, the parent or parent-surrogate was asked for permission to have the child's teacher complete the TRF. If permission was granted, the TRF was sent to the teacher with the signed permission, a postpaid return envelope, and an explanatory letter offering $10 for returning the completed TRF. If the child had more than one regular teacher, the parent was asked to name the teacher who knew the child best. Of the 2,113 5- to 18-year-olds whose parents gave permission, completed TRFs were obtained for 1,613 (76.3%).

A normative sample was constructed by drawing from the pool of 5- to 18-year-olds all those who had not received mental health services or special remedial school classes within the preceding 12 months. This was done to provide a normative sample of children who were considered to be "healthy" in the sense that they had not recently received professional help for behavioral/emotional problems. This criterion may, of course, fail to exclude children who have significant problems that have not received professional attention for various reasons, including lack of parental concern. On the other hand, the exclusion criterion of referral for help may inadvertently exclude children who do not have significant problems but whose parents might be overconcerned. Both these types of errors would reduce our ability to identify items and scale scores that discriminate between "healthy" and "disturbed" children.

Despite the inevitable error variance in our definitions of both "healthy" and "disturbed" children, most TRF scale and item scores discriminated very well between referred and nonreferred children, as documented in Chapters 6 and 7. If a more accurate criterion of truly "healthy" versus truly "disturbed" could be applied in large representative samples like ours, still better discrimination might be found. However, as detailed elsewhere (Achenbach & Edelbrock, 1981), other criteria for distinguishing between normal and deviant children have not functioned better than referral status.

Table 2-1 summarizes the demographic characteristics of the 5- to 18-year-olds who comprised the TRF normative samples, after excluding those who had received mental health services or special education classes during the previous 12 months.

ASSIGNMENT OF PERCENTILES AND *T* SCORES

Figure 2-1 displays the academic and adaptive portion of the TRF hand-scored profile for 12-year-old Raymond. As can be seen in Figure 2-1, percentiles are displayed on the left side of the adaptive functioning profile and *T* scores are displayed on the right side. The percentiles enable the user to compare a pupil's raw score on each item and scale with percentiles for the normative sample of the pupil's sex and age range. The *T* scores, which are automatically computed by the TRF computer-scoring program, provide a metric that is similar for all scales. (The remainder of this section can be skipped by readers uninterested in how *T* scores were assigned. Chapter 10 discusses the use of raw scores versus *T* scores for statistical purposes.)

The percentiles indicated on the 1991 TRF profile were derived according to a procedure designed to produce smoother, more normal distributions of percentile scores than were generated for the pre-1991 profile. According to this procedure, a raw score that falls at a particular percentage of the cumulative frequency distribution is assumed to span all the

Table 2-1
Demographic Distribution of TRF Normative Sample

		Boys		Girls		
		5-11	*12-18*	*5-11*	*12-18*	*Combined[b]*
N =		334	309	379	369	1,391
SES[a]						
Upper		37%	36%	43%	39%	39%
Middle		47	42	43	41	43
Lower		17	22	15	20	18
Mean Scores		5.7	5.5	5.9	5.6	5.7
SD of Scores		2.2	2.2	2.2	2.2	2.2
Ethnicity						
White		75%	76%	77%	77%	76%
Black		14	13	16	12	14
Hispanic		8	8	6	7	7
Other		4	3	1	4	3
Region						
Northeast		22%	21%	24%	24%	23%
North Central		26	31	26	27	27
South		31	30	34	31	32
West		21	18	16	18	18
TRF Respondent						
Teacher		99%	96%	100%	96%	98%
Counselor		0	3	0	2	1
Other		1	2	0	2	1

[a]Hollingshead (1975) 9-step scale for parental occupation, using the higher status occupation if both parents were wage earners; scores 1 - 3.5 = lower; 4 - 6.5 = middle; 7 - 9 = upper. If occupational level was unclear, the mean of the two most likely scores was used, resulting in some half-step scores, such as 3.5.
[b]Scores for the combined samples are unweighted means of the 4 sex/age groups.

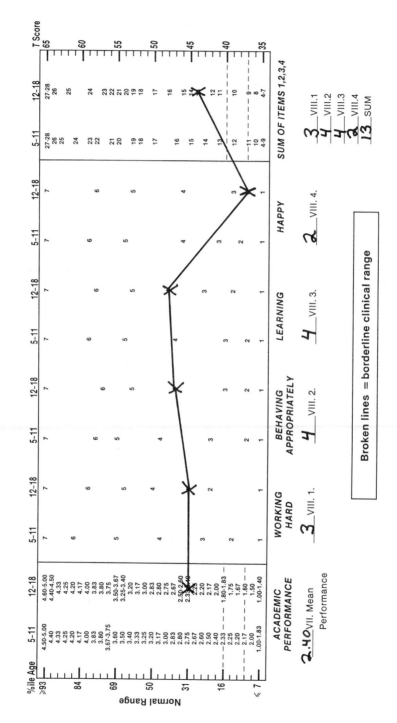

Figure 2-1. Hand-scored TRF adaptive functioning profile for 12-year-old Raymond.

next lower percentiles down to the percentile occupied by the next lower raw score in the distribution (Crocker & Algina, 1986). To represent this span of percentiles, each raw score is assigned to the midpoint of the percentiles that it spans. For example, 20.2% of 12- to 18-year-old boys obtained a raw score of 11 or lower on the sum of the four adaptive functioning items (shown on the right side of the profile in Figure 2-1). The next higher raw score, 12, was obtained by 3.0% of the boys. The *cumulative percent* of boys obtaining a raw score of 11 or lower was thus 20.2%, while the cumulative percent obtaining a raw score of 12 or lower was 20.2% + 3.0% = 23.2%. The interval from raw score 11 to raw score 12 thus spanned from a cumulative percent of 20.2% to a cumulative percent of 23.2%. To represent this interval in terms of a percentile at the midpoint of the interval, we took the cumulative percent at the top of the interval (23.2%) and subtracted the cumulative percent at the bottom of the interval (20.2%), i.e., 23.2% minus 20.2% = 3.0%. To obtain the midpoint, we then divided this difference in half and added the result to the lower percent, i.e., 20.2 + 1.5 = 21.7. This corresponds to the following formula provided by Crocker and Algina (1986, p. 439):

$$P = \frac{cf_l + .5(f_i)}{N} \times 100\%$$

where P = percentile; cf_l is the cumulative frequency for all scores lower than the score of interest; f_i is the frequency of scores in the interval of interest; and N is the number in the sample.

After obtaining the midpoint percentile in this way, we used the procedure provided by Abramowitz and Stegun (1968) to assign a normalized T score of 42 to the 21.7th percentile for the raw score of 12. In Figure 2-1, the raw score of 12 is therefore on the same line as the T score of 42 listed on the right side of the profile.

The main effect of using the midpoint percentile rather than the cumulative percentile on the syndrome scales was to provide a smoother, less skewed, and more differentiated basis for T scores. We truncated the assignment of lower T scores at 35 and upper T scores at 65 to reduce gaps and to prevent overinterpretations of differences at the extremes of the distributions. The gaps between scores displayed on the adaptive functioning portion of the 1991 TRF profile are therefore smaller than those displayed on the pre-1991 TRF profile.

Looking again at Raymond's profile in Figure 2-1, you can see that Raymond obtained a mean score of 2.40 on the Academic Performance scale. The left side of the profile shows that a raw score of 2.40 on the Academic Performance scale falls at the 31st percentile for 12- to 18-year-old boys. As shown on the right side of the profile, this is equivalent to a T score of 45, which is toward the middle of the normal range. On the four adaptive characteristics, Raymond received scores of 3 for Working Hard, 4 for Behaving Appropriately and Learning, and 2 for Happy. By looking to the left of the profile, we can determine the approximate percentiles for these scores, and by looking to the right of the profile, we can determine the T score for each one. Table 2-2 presents the mean, standard deviation, and standard error of the raw scores and T scores obtained by our normative samples on each adaptive functioning scale.

SUMMARY

TRF ratings of academic performance, four adaptive characteristics, and the sum of the four adaptive characteristics are scored on the adaptive functioning portion of the TRF profile. The procedures for assigning percentiles and T scores to the 1991 adaptive functioning scale scores were detailed and illustrated. The normative samples for the 1991 TRF profile scales were described and their mean raw and T scores for each scale were presented.

Table 2-2
Academic and Adaptive Scores for TRF Normative Samples

Scale	Boys 5-11	Boys 12-18	Girls 5-11	Girls 12-18
N^b = 334		309	379	369
Academic Performance				
Raw Score				
Mean	3.2	3.0	3.3	3.4
SD	.8	1.0	.8	1.0
SE[a]	.0	.1	.0	.1
T Score				
Mean	50.2	50.0	49.9	51.1
SD	8.5	8.9	8.7	9.4
SE[a]	.5	.5	.4	.5
Working Hard				
Raw Score				
Mean	4.1	4.0	4.7	4.9
SD	1.6	1.9	1.6	1.7
SE[a]	.1	.1	.1	.1
T Score				
Mean	50.2	50.0	50.4	50.2
SD	8.5	8.9	8.8	8.4
SE[a]	.5	.5	.5	.4
Behaving Appropriately				
Raw Score				
Mean	4.3	4.6	5.1	5.3
SD	1.7	1.6	1.5	1.6
SE[a]	.1	.1	.1	.1
T Score				
Mean	50.4	50.3	50.1	50.2
SD	8.8	8.7	8.5	7.8
SE[a]	.5	.5	.4	.4
Learning				
Raw Score				
Mean	4.5	4.3	4.8	5.0
SD	1.4	1.7	1.4	1.5
SE[a]	.1	.1	.1	.1
T Score				
Mean	50.2	49.9	50.0	50.2
SD	8.3	8.5	8.7	8.4
SE[a]	.5	.5	.4	.4

Table 2-2 (Continued)

Scale	Boys 5-11	Boys 12-18	Girls 5-11	Girls 12-18
Happy				
Raw Score				
Mean	4.6	4.6	5.0	4.9
SD	1.3	1.5	1.4	1.5
SE[a]	.1	.1	.1	.1
T Score				
Mean	50.5	50.0	50.6	50.7
SD	7.8	8.5	8.2	8.4
SE[a]	.4	.5	.4	.4
Total Adaptive				
Raw Score				
Mean	17.5	17.4	19.6	20.1
SD	5.1	6.0	5.0	5.5
SE[a]	.3	.3	.3	.3
T Score				
Mean	49.9	50.2	50.0	50.1
SD	8.7	8.7	8.7	8.7
SE[a]	.5	.5	.5	.5

[a]SE = standard error of the mean.
[b]Ns vary because of missing data for some scales.

Chapter 3
Syndrome and Total Problem Scales

Beside describing children in terms of many specific items, the TRF is also designed to identify syndromes of problems that tend to occur together. In fact, a primary reason for developing the TRF was to provide an empirical foundation for identifying syndromes from which to construct a taxonomy of childhood disorders. The word *syndrome* refers to problems that tend to occur together, without implying any particular model for the nature or causes of disorders. Rather than imposing *a priori* assumptions about what syndromes exist, we derived syndromes quantitatively from TRF problem items scored by teachers for children who were referred for mental health or special education services. (Findings for the pre-1991 edition of the TRF profile have been reported by Achenbach & Edelbrock, 1986, and Edelbrock & Achenbach, 1984.)

To derive the syndromes, we applied principal components analyses to the correlations among items. Like factor analysis, principal components analysis is used to identify groups of items whose scores covary with each other. However, in factor analysis, the obtained correlations among items are reduced to reflect only the variance each item has in common with all other items. The estimate of the item's "communality" (the variance it has in common with all other items) typically consists of the square of the item's multiple correlation with all other items. In principal components analysis, by contrast, the obtained correlation of each item with each other item is taken at face value rather than being reduced according to an estimate of communality.

Because we wanted to focus on the associations that were actually obtained among items in large samples, we did not want the associations among particular items to be differentially reduced by the degree to which the items happened to correlate with all other items. When the number of items is as large as we used, the results of principal components analyses are generally similar to the results of principal factor analyses in any event (Gorsuch, 1983).

PRE-1991 SYNDROMES

To reflect possible sex and age differences in the prevalence and patterning of problems, we performed separate principal components analyses for each sex within particular age ranges. For the pre-1991 editions of the TRF profiles, the age ranges were 6 to 11 and 12 to 16. We analyzed all items that were reported to be present for at least 5% of a referred sample of a particular sex and age. This number ranged from 113 to 114 items for the four sex/age groups.

We applied orthogonal (varimax) and oblique (direct quartimin) rotations to the largest 8 to 15 components obtained for each sex/age group. We then compared all the orthogonal and oblique rotations within each sex/age group to identify sets of problems that tended to remain together in most of the analyses. Next, we chose the rotation that included the most representative sets of problem items found for a particular sex/age group. These items formed the basis for the syndrome scales for that sex/age group. Note that the pre-1991 syndrome scales for each sex/age group were based directly on the rotated components for that sex/age group alone, whether or not similar syndromes were found for other sex/age groups. Analogous procedures were followed in developing the pre-1991 syndrome scales for each sex/age group on the CBCL and YSR.

In deriving the pre-1991 syndromes, we sought to capture possible differences in the patterning of problems for different sex/age groups, as seen by different informants. Our analyses of each group yielded some syndromes that were similar among different sex/age groups scored by different informants.

However, the exact composition of these syndromes varied among the sex/age groups and informants.

The variations may have been partly due to some differences in the items that were analyzed, as even within a particular instrument, such as the TRF, the items that failed to meet the 5% prevalence criterion varied among the sex/age groups. Differences in the item lists rated by different informants could have contributed to differences in the syndromes obtained from the TRF, CBCL, and YSR. Chance differences among samples could also have contributed to variations among syndromes.

When the focus was on each sex/age group as seen by each informant taken separately, the differences among syndromes did not pose major problems. Because the overall list of items on a particular instrument was the same for scoring all sex/age groups on that instrument, children of both sexes and different ages could be compared on each specific item, as well as on total scores computed by summing all items. By using standard scores derived from normative samples, different sex/age groups could also be compared with each other on those of the syndromes that were fairly similar from one sex/age group to another.

DERIVATION OF THE 1991 SYNDROMES

As the development and applications of our instruments have advanced, it has become more important to coordinate assessment of children of both sexes in different age ranges and as seen from different perspectives. A more uniform set of syndrome scales across sex/age groups and instruments would make it easier for users to keep track of the syndromes being assessed. The common elements of syndromes derived from the different instruments for multiple sex/age groups would also provide the basis for taxonomic constructs that transcend specific instruments. Such constructs would serve as foci for research and theory from diverse perspectives.

To improve the coordination of assessment for both sexes across the age range spanned by the TRF, we performed new principal components analyses of clinical samples of each sex at ages 5 to 11 and 12 to 18. These samples included TRFs that had been analyzed for the previous edition of the profile (Achenbach & Edelbrock, 1986), plus additional TRFs obtained for children referred for mental health or special education services since then.

The subjects were seen in 58 settings, including special education programs, guidance clinics, private psychiatric and psychological practices, community mental health centers, university child psychiatric and psychological services, and residential treatment settings. Located throughout the eastern, southern, and midwestern United States, the settings provided a broad distribution of socioeconomic, demographic, and other client characteristics that should minimize selective factors affecting the caseloads of individual services. On Hollingshead's (1975) 9-step scale for parental occupation, the mean SES was 4.8 (SD = 2.1), averaged across the distributions for the four sex/age groups. Ethnic distribution averaged across the four sex/age groups was 89.2% white, 8.7% black, and 2.2% other. (The following sections can be skipped by readers uninterested in how the 1991 syndromes were derived.)

Principal Components Analyses

Two principal components analyses were performed on the sample for each sex/age group. One analysis resembled the analyses used to develop the previous edition of the profile. This analysis employed all problem items that were reported for at least 5% of a particular sex/age group. The open-ended items, *56h. Other physical problems* and *113. Other problems*, were not included, because their content varied across subjects according to what the respondents wrote in. Because our focus was now on syndromes that were common to multiple sex/age groups, we also included the following items that were reported for <5% of a particular sample but that had loaded highly on syndromes previously found for most sex/age groups: Boys 5-11—*101. Truancy*; girls 5-11—none; boys 12-18—*5. Behaves like opposite sex, 70. Sees things, 110. Wishes to be opposite sex*; girls 12-18—none. Table 3-1 lists the sample sizes and the items that were excluded from the analyses for each sex/age group.

Table 3-1
Low Prevalence Items Omitted from
TRF Principal Components Analyses[a]

Group	N	Items
Boys 5-11	926	51. Dizzy; 56e. Skin problems; 56g. Vomiting; 105. Alcohol, drugs.
Girls 5-11	697	56g. Vomiting; 105. Alcohol, drugs.
Boys 12-18	647	56e. Skin problems; 56g. Vomiting.
Girls 12-18	545	28. Eats things that aren't food.

[a]Items *56h. Other physical problems* and *113. Other problems not listed above* were also excluded from all principal components analyses.

The second principal components analysis for each sex/age group was designed to identify syndromes that had counterparts in ratings by multiple informants. This analysis therefore employed only the 89 problem items that have counterparts on the CBCL and YSR, as well as being on the TRF.

Rotations of Principal Components

After performing principal components analyses, we subjected the largest 7 to 15 components from each analysis to orthogonal (varimax) rotations. (Rotations of principal components are transformations of their item loadings designed to approximate the ideal of "simple structure"—that is, to divide all the items that were analyzed into relatively few tightly knit groups of strongly interrelated items.)

In all the analyses for the pre-1991 syndromes, the orthogonal (varimax) rotations had provided more stable and representative solutions than the oblique (direct quartimin) rotations. For this reason, and to minimize correlations among syndromes, only varimax rotations were performed to identify the 1991 syndromes. Although the varimax criterion for simple structure avoids correlations among rotated components, this does not preclude correlations among the sets of high loading items that are retained from the rotated components to form syndrome scales. In fact, as shown in Appendix C, the final syndrome scales do correlate positively with each other.

For each sex/age group, the 7- to 15-component rotations were examined to identify sets of items that consistently grouped together with high loadings on a rotated component. Four to five rotations were selected that included representative versions of these components. The items loading ≥.30 on these components were then listed side-by-side to identify the version of each component that included the maximum number of high loading items which also loaded highly on the other versions. (As done for the pre-1991 syndromes, we retained items loading ≥.30 for all syndromes except the one designated as *Aggressive Behavior*, for which the large number of high loading items argued for retaining items with loadings ≥.40. Items that loaded ≥.40 on the Aggressive syndrome and ≥.30 on a second syndrome were retained only for the second syndrome.)

After selecting the two to three best versions of each rotated component, we identified the rotation that included the largest proportion of the best versions of each component. The versions of the rotated components found in this rotation were used to represent the syndromes for the sex/age group for which the analysis was done.

Example of Syndrome Identification. As an example, we performed a principal components analysis of 114 problem items scored for the TRFs of 926 5- to 11-year-old boys, excluding the four low prevalence items listed in Table 3-1. We then identified syndromes of items that tended to occur together, as reflected by their high loadings on a particular component. We selected the 10-, 11-, 12-, and 13-component rotations as including the best examples of these syndromes of high loading items.

One syndrome was designated as *Anxious/Depressed*, because the items loading ≥.30 all appeared to reflect anxiety and depression. From the versions of this syndrome found in the 10-, 11-, 12-, and 13-component rotations, we listed items that loaded ≥.30 on any of the four versions. We found that three of the four versions had exactly the same 14 items loading ≥.30. On the remaining version, an additional item loaded >.30. Based on the Anxious/Depressed syndrome, the three rotations that produced identical sets of high loading items all became equal candidates for retention. The same procedure was followed for each of the other syndromes that appeared in multiple rotations of the components for 5- to 11-year-old boys.

When we tabulated the number of syndromes whose best versions occurred in each rotation, we found that the 11-component rotation had "best" versions of seven syndromes and a "second best" version of one syndrome. Because this was a greater concentration of best versions than found in any other rotation, the 11-component rotation was retained as the basis for the syndromes identified for 5- to 11-year-old boys. As explained in the following sections, the syndromes selected from the analyses of 114 items for 5- to 11-year-old boys contributed only a small part to the final selection of items for the 1991 TRF syndrome scales.

Analysis of 89 Common Items

Recall now that a second principal components analysis was performed on the TRF sample for each sex/age group. To identify "cross-informant" syndromes that were common to the TRF, CBCL, and YSR, the second principal components analyses employed only the 89 problem items that are common to the three instruments, minus the low frequency items listed in Table 3-1. Varimax rotations were performed on the largest 7 to 15 components obtained for each sex/age group. The procedures outlined earlier were then used to identify the syndromes that would serve as the TRF candidates for the cross-informant syndromes. We thus obtained two sets of syndromes for each sex/age group. For boys 5 to 11, for example, one set was derived from the analysis of 114 items, while the second set was derived from the analysis of the 89 common items, minus the low frequency items shown in Table 3-1.

Derivation of Core Syndromes

The syndromes derived from the two sets of analyses for each sex/age group represent two alternative ways of viewing patterns of co-occurring problems. The analyses of all the items specific to the TRF might detect patterns that are not detectible in the subset of items common to the TRF, CBCL, and YSR. The analyses of the common items, on the other hand, might identify patterns that are also detectible in CBCL and YSR ratings.

To determine whether particular syndromes were evident only in the analyses of the full set of TRF items, we compared the syndromes obtained from these analyses with the syndromes obtained from the analyses of the subset of common items. Eight syndromes were found in the analyses of both the full set of items and the common-item subset. Table 3-2 lists the

names of the syndromes and the mean of their eigenvalues
obtained in the varimax rotation of the full set of items.

Table 3-2
Syndromes Retained from Principal
Components/Varimax Analyses of the TRF

Internalizing	Neither Int nor Ext	Externalizing
Withdrawn (4.48)	Social (3.42) Problems	Delinquent (3.10) Behavior
Somatic (3.78) Complaints	Thought (3.48) Problems	Aggressive (16.81) Behavior
Anxious/ (5.83) Depressed	Attention (7.12) Problems	

Note. Internalizing and Externalizing groupings were derived from second-order
analyses, as explained in Chapter 4. Mean of the eigenvalues for all sex/age
groups in which the syndrome was found is shown in parentheses.

There were some differences between the items comprising
the versions of syndromes obtained from the analyses of the
full set and those obtained from the common-item subset.
There were also differences among the versions of each
syndrome found for different sex/age groups. To identify *core*
syndromes that underlay these variations, we listed side-by-side
the items of the versions of a syndrome obtained from each
sex/age group in both the full set and the common-item
analyses. We then determined which items were found in the
syndrome for a majority of the sex/age groups in which the
syndrome was obtained. The Somatic Complaints syndrome,
for example, was found for all four sex/age groups. We
therefore constructed the core Somatic Complaints syndrome
from items that were found in versions of this syndrome for at
least three of the four sex/age groups. An item was counted as
present for a particular sex/age group if it was found in either
the full set or common-item version of the syndrome for that
group. (Item *105. Uses alcohol or drugs for nonmedical*

purposes was retained for the core *Delinquent Behavior* syndrome because it loaded very highly for 12-18-year-olds of both sexes, although it was too uncommon among younger children for inclusion in their principal components analyses.) The core syndromes were used in the following ways:

1. They provided the items for the 1991 syndrome scales. Thus, scales were constructed for eight syndromes found in both the full set and common-item subset. The items comprising the core syndrome are used to score all the sex/age groups that are scored for that syndrome.

2. The core versions of the syndromes found in the common-item subset were compared with common-item core syndromes from the CBCL and YSR to identify syndromes that were similar in two or more instruments.

Cross-Informant Syndromes

A major aim of the 1991 profiles is to provide common foci for assessing children from the perspectives of teacher-, parent-, and self-reports. These common foci consist of syndromes that were identified as having counterparts in the principal components analyses of the TRF, CBCL, and YSR. Core syndromes were constructed from the syndromes derived from the CBCL and YSR by the method just described for the TRF (details are provided by Achenbach, 1991b, 1991c).

To identify items that were common to the core syndromes of two or more informants, we made side-by-side lists of the items comprising the corresponding core syndromes from the different instruments. Items that were found on core syndromes for at least two of the three instruments were used to form a *cross-informant syndrome construct*. For example, items of the core Somatic Complaints syndromes derived from the TRF, CBCL, and YSR were listed side-by-side. Nine items were found to be common to the core Somatic Complaints syndrome from at least two of the three instruments. These nine items were used to define a cross-informant syndrome construct which could be assessed via the Somatic Complaints scales of the TRF, CBCL, and YSR.

The term "construct" is used to indicate that the common items represent an hypothetical variable. In statistical language, the term "latent variable" is used for variables of this sort. Because none of the core syndromes for the individual instruments included any additional items, the Somatic Complaints scales for all three instruments have the same nine items, although they are normed separately for the different informants, as described later.

For some cross-informant constructs, the core syndrome of a particular instrument did include items beside those that qualified for the cross-informant construct. Because these items were associated with the syndrome in ratings by a particular type of informant, they were retained for the syndrome scale to be scored by that type of informant. As an example, for the cross-informant construct designated as *Anxious/Depressed*, the TRF core syndrome included item *47. Overconforms to rules.* This item is not on the CBCL or YSR, because it is more likely to be observed by teachers than by parents or to be self-reported by youths. Because it was associated with the TRF Anxious/Depressed syndrome in a majority of the sex/age groups, it is scored on the TRF Anxious/Depressed scale even though it is not part of the cross-informant construct and is not scored on the CBCL or YSR Anxious/Depressed scales. Other items were also retained on particular scales for one instrument to capture aspects of a syndrome that might be evident to only one type of informant. Table 3-3 summarizes the steps in constructing the 1991 syndrome scales.

Table 3-3
Steps in Deriving 1991 TRF Syndrome Scales

---

1. Two sets of principal components analyses were performed on TRF problem items for referred children of each sex at ages 5-11 and 12-18.

   a. Set 1—principal components analysis of all but low prevalence TRF problem items.

   b. Set 2—principal components analysis of 89 problem items common to TRF, YSR, CBCL.

2. Varimax rotations of 7 to 15 components from each analysis.

3. Identification of groups of items that remained together throughout multiple rotations.

4. Selection of rotation that included the largest proportion of the best versions of groups of co-occurring items.

5. Derivation of *core syndromes* from items found in the versions of a syndrome for most sex/age groups.

6. Derivation of *cross-informant syndrome constructs* from items common to core syndromes for at least two of the three instruments (TRF, YSR, CBCL).

7. Construction of TRF syndrome scales consisting of TRF items for the eight cross-informant constructs.

8. Assignment of normalized T scores based on percentiles of normative samples, separately for each sex at ages 5-11 and 12-18.

PROFILES FOR SCORING
THE 1991 SYNDROMES

The 1991 profiles for the TRF, CBCL, and YSR display the items of the eight cross-informant syndromes that are scored from the respective type of informant. To facilitate comparison among reports by the different informants, the syndromes are arranged in the same order on all three profiles. A cross-informant computer program is available that scores and compares data from any combination of father-, mother-, youth-, and teacher-reports (details are provided by Achenbach, 1991a).

For users who have access to only one type of informant, programs are also available that score only the TRF, CBCL, or YSR. The syndromes that were found in ratings by only one type of informant are not displayed on the profiles, because they comprise relatively rare problems and their distributions of scores do not lend themselves to a profile approach. However, the computer-scoring programs compute total scores and *T* scores for these scales, and the hand-scoring profiles provide spaces to enter the scores for them.

Figure 3-1 shows the problem scales portion of a computer-scored profile completed for 12-year-old Raymond (Appendix A provides detailed hand-scoring instructions.) The eight syndromes displayed on the profile have counterparts that bear the same names on the 1991 profiles for the CBCL and YSR. The names are intended as descriptive summaries of the items comprising the syndromes, rather than being diagnostic labels. Chapter 4 presents the basis for designating scales I-III as Internalizing and scales VII-VIII as Externalizing.

The items comprising each scale are listed under the title of the scale. A total scale score is computed by summing the 1s and 2s for the scale's items that were scored as describing the child. Asterisks indicate items on the TRF version of a cross-informant syndrome scale that are not on the CBCL or YSR versions. On syndrome scale *III. Anxious/Depressed*, for example, the asterisk beside Item *47. Conforms* indicates that it was included in the core syndrome derived from the principal components analyses of the four sex/age groups scored on the TRF, but not on the core syndromes scored on the YSR or TRF. Item 47 is therefore scored on the TRF *Anxious/Depressed* scale but not on the CBCL or YSR *Anxious/Depressed* scales. The computer program prints out scores at the

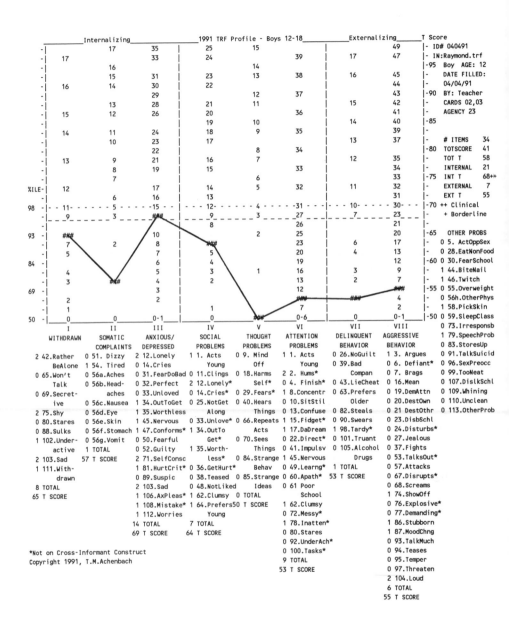

Figure 3-1. Computer-scored problem profile for 12-year-old Raymond.

bottom of each scale that indicate how a child's scale score compares with scores obtained by normative samples of children. Later sections of this chapter explain how the *T* scores were assigned. Items that are not scored on syndrome scales I-VIII are listed to the right of the profile under the heading *Other Problems*. These items do not constitute a separate scale, but they are included in the TRF total problem score.

As detailed in Chapter 4, scores for Internalizing and Externalizing are computed by summing Scales I-III and VII-VIII, respectively. The computer program prints raw scores and *T* scores for Internalizing and Externalizing to the right of the profile, as shown in Figure 3-1. Because Item *103. Unhappy, sad, or depressed* is scored both on Scale I and Scale III, its score is subtracted from the sum of Scales I, II, and III in order to avoid counting it twice in the Internalizing score. No items are included on both an Internalizing and External-izing scale.

The total problem score is computed by summing all problem items on pages 3 and 4 of the TRF. If the teacher rated more than one problem item for *113. Other problems*, only the problem receiving the highest score is counted toward the total problem score. For example, if one additional problem was rated 1 and a second additional problem was rated 2, 2 is added to the total problem score. The computer program prints the raw score and *T* score for the total problem score to the right of the profile, as shown in Figure 3-1.

ASSIGNING NORMALIZED *T* SCORES TO SYNDROME SCALES

(This section can be skipped by readers uninterested in how *T* scores were assigned.)

Lowest T Scores

For each syndrome scale, we computed percentiles using the same procedure and normative samples as were described in Chapter 2 for the adaptive functioning scales. On some syndrome scales, more than 50% of the normative sample obtained scores of 0 or 1. On other syndrome scales, much smaller percentages of the normative sample obtained very low scores. If we assigned normalized T scores solely on the basis of percentiles, some scales would start at much lower T scores than other scales would. When displayed on a profile, the different starting points for the scales could lead to misleading impressions. For example, if a child obtained a raw score of 0 on a scale that started at a T score of 28 and a raw score of 0 on a scale that started at a T score of 50, it might appear that the child scored higher on the second scale than on the first. Yet, the child had no problems on either scale.

To avoid misleading impressions of this sort and to prevent over-interpretation of differences among scores in the low normal range, we truncated the assignment of T scores to the syndrome scales. Based on the midpoint percentiles, no syndrome scales would have required starting at a T score higher than 50, which is equivalent to the 50th percentile. To equalize the starting points of all the syndrome scales, we assigned a T score of 50 to all raw scores that fell at midpoint percentiles ≤50. As an example, on Scale *V. Thought Problems* for boys 12-18, only a raw score of 0 fell ≤50th percentile. On Scale *VI. Attention Problems*, by contrast, raw scores of 0-6 were all ≤50th percentile. All these scores were therefore assigned a T score of 50, as shown in Figure 3-1.

The assignment of a T score of 50 to several raw scores reduces the differentiation among low scores on scales such as the *Attention Problems* scale. Loss of this differentiation is of little clinical importance, because it involves small differences that are all at the low end of the normal range. If differentiation at the low end is nevertheless desired for assessing differences that are within the normal range, raw scale scores may be used in place of T scores. For statistical analyses, raw scores are usually preferable, because they directly reflect all differences among individuals without any truncation or other transformations.

On scales comprising low prevalence items, a large percentage of the normative sample obtained the second lowest possible raw score on the scale. This produced a large gap between the percentiles of the lowest score and the second lowest score. If the second lowest score qualified for a T score >55, we limited the gap between the T score of 50 and the next T score by assigning it a T score half way between 50 and the third lowest T score. On the Thought Problems scale of the profile shown in Figure 3-1, for example, the second lowest T score would have been 59 if we based it directly on the midpoint percentile. However, by assigning this T score to a point half way between 50 and the third lowest T score, we assigned the second lowest score a $T = 58$, thus reducing the gap slightly between the lowest and second lowest T score.

Highest T Scores

Most children in the normative samples obtained scores that were well below the maximum possible on each syndrome scale. It was therefore impossible to base T scores on percentiles at the high end of the syndrome scales. On the *Attention Problems* scale shown in Figure 3-1, for example, the maximum possible score is 40, but 98% of the normative sample of 12- to 18-year-old boys obtained scores ≤31. Furthermore, most of the scores from 31 to 40 were not obtained by any boys in the normative sample. Basing T scores on percentiles above the 98th percentile would thus not really reflect differences among scores obtained by boys in the normative sample. We therefore based T scores on percentiles only up to a T score of 70, which approximates the 97.7th percentile (Abramowitz & Stegun, 1968).

For the highest scores on the syndrome scales, we assigned T scores from 71 to 100 in as many increments as there were remaining raw scores on the scale. For example, on the *Attention Problems* scale for boys 12-18, the raw score of 31 was assigned a T score of 70. Because there are 20 items on the scale, the maximum possible score is 40 (i.e., if a boy received a score of 2 on all 20 items, his raw scale score would be 40). There are 30 intervals from 71 to 100, but only 9 possible raw scores from 31 through 40. To assign T scores to the 9 raw scores, we divided 30 by 9. Because $30/9 = 3.33$, T scores were assigned to raw scores in intervals of 3.33. Thus, a raw score of 32 was assigned a T score of $70 + 3.33 = 73.33$, rounded off to 73. A raw score of 33 was assigned a T score of $73.33 + 3.33 = 76.66$, rounded off to 77, and so on.

Because of the skewed raw score distribution, truncation of low scores at $T = 50$, and assignment of high T scores in equal intervals, the mean T scores of the syndrome scales are above 50 and their standard deviations are below 10. They thus do not conform to the mean of 50 and standard deviation of 10 expected when normal distributions are transformed directly into T scores. The means and standard deviations also differ between normative and clinical samples, of course. Table 3-4 presents the means, standard deviations, and standard errors for the normative samples. Appendix B presents the corresponding data for all TRF scales in demographically matched referred and nonreferred samples of each sex at ages 5-11 and 12-18.

ASSIGNING NORMALIZED T SCORES TO TOTAL PROBLEM SCORES

We based normalized T scores on midpoint percentiles of the total problem score in the same way as described for the syndrome scales, with the following two differences:

Table 3-4
Problem Scale Scores for TRF Normative Samples

Scale	Boys 5-11	Boys 12-18	Girls 5-11	Girls 12-18
N =	334	309	379	369
Withdrawn				
Raw Score				
Mean	1.8	2.1	1.8	1.8
SD	2.5	3.0	2.6	2.6
SE[a]	.1	.2	.1	.1
T Score				
Mean	54.2	54.1	54.0	54.0
SD	6.3	6.4	6.3	6.2
SE[a]	.3	.4	.3	.3
Somatic Complaints				
Raw Score				
Mean	.5	.6	.7	.4
SD	1.4	1.5	1.6	1.0
SE[a]	.1	.1	.1	.1
T Score				
Mean	52.9	53.0	52.9	52.2
SD	6.2	6.1	5.9	5.2
SE[a]	.3	.3	.3	.3
Anxious/Depressed				
Raw Score				
Mean	3.2	2.8	3.1	3.0
SD	3.7	3.9	4.0	4.1
SE[a]	.2	.2	.2	.2
T Score				
Mean	54.1	54.0	54.1	54.0
SD	5.9	5.9	6.1	6.1
SE[a]	.3	.3	.3	.3
Social Problems				
Raw Score				
Mean	1.8	1.9	1.6	1.4
SD	2.7	3.2	2.7	2.7
SE[a]	.1	.2	.1	.1
T Score				
Mean	54.1	54.2	53.9	54.0
SD	6.1	6.1	5.9	6.2
SE[a]	.3	.3	.3	.3

Table 3-4 (Continued)

Scale	Boys 5-11	Boys 12-18	Girls 5-11	Girls 12-18
Thought Problems				
Raw Score				
Mean	.4	.4	.3	.3
SD	.8	1.0	.8	.8
SE[a]	.0	.1	.0	.0
T Score				
Mean	52.4	52.4	52.2	52.1
SD	5.3	5.4	5.2	5.0
SE[a]	.3	.3	.3	.3
Attention Problems				
Raw Score				
Mean	8.7	8.7	5.5	4.7
SD	8.5	9.1	6.9	6.5
SE[a]	.5	.5	.4	.3
T Score				
Mean	54.1	54.2	54.1	54.0
SD	6.2	6.4	6.3	6.1
SE[a]	.3	.4	.3	.3
Delinquent Behavior				
Raw Score				
Mean	1.3	1.6	.8	1.0
SD	1.8	2.7	1.4	1.6
SE[a]	.1	.2	.1	.1
T Score				
Mean	54.0	54.2	53.7	53.8
SD	5.7	6.5	6.0	5.6
SE[a]	.3	.4	.3	.3
Aggressive Behavior				
Raw Score				
Mean	6.0	5.5	3.5	3.2
SD	8.2	8.3	5.8	6.4
SE[a]	.4	.5	.3	.3
T Score				
Mean	54.0	54.2	54.0	54.1
SD	6.1	6.8	5.9	6.4
SE[a]	.3	.4	.3	.3

Table 3-4 (Continued)

Scale	Boys 5-11	Boys 12-18	Girls 5-11	Girls 12-18
Internalizing				
Raw Score				
Mean	5.3	5.2	5.5	5.0
SD	5.6	6.7	6.4	6.4
SE[a]	.3	.4	.3	.3
T Score				
Mean	50.2	50.5	50.3	50.3
SD	9.7	9.4	9.5	9.4
SE[a]	.5	.5	.5	.5
Externalizing				
Raw Score				
Mean	7.2	7.1	4.2	4.2
SD	9.6	10.5	6.8	7.6
SE[a]	.5	.6	.4	.4
T Score				
Mean	50.3	50.7	50.7	50.7
SD	9.4	9.5	8.8	8.9
SE[a]	.5	.5	.5	.5
Total Problems				
Raw Score				
Mean	23.5	23.8	17.2	15.6
SD	21.9	26.1	19.0	19.9
SE[a]	1.2	1.5	1.0	1.0
T Score				
Mean	50.1	50.3	50.2	50.3
SD	9.8	10.1	9.8	10.0
SE[a]	.5	.6	.5	.5

[a]SE = standard error of the mean.

1. The total number of problem items is much greater than the number of items on any syndrome scale, and at least some problems are reported for most children. Consequently, very few children in our normative samples obtained extremely low total problem scores. It was therefore unnecessary to set a minimum T score at which to group low raw scores as we did for the syndrome scales. Instead, we based normalized T scores directly on percentiles of the distribution of total problem scores obtained by our normative samples, up to the 97.7th percentile ($T = 70$).

2. No child in either our normative or clinical samples obtained a total problem score approaching the maximum possible of 240. If we assigned T scores above 70 by dividing all the top raw scores into the 30 intervals from 71 to 100, we would have compressed scores actually obtained by our clinical samples into a narrow range of T scores. We would also have assigned raw scores above those actually obtained to a broad range of T scores. For example, the highest total score obtained in our sample of referred 5- to 11-year-old girls was 151. If we had assigned T scores in equal intervals from 70 to 100, only 13 T scores would have been allocated to the range of 71 raw scores above $T = 70$ actually found in our referred sample, whereas 17 T scores would have been allocated to the 89 raw scores above those actually found.

   To enable the upper T scores to reflect differences among the raw scores that are most likely to occur, we assigned a T score of 89 for each sex/age group to the mean of the five highest raw scores found in the referred sample on which the principal components analyses were performed. (In contrast to the use of the single highest score in the pre-1991 profiles, we used the mean of the five highest scores to reduce the effect of single extreme outliers.) The raw scores ranging from $T = 70$ to the mean of the five highest scores were then assigned T scores in equal intervals from 71 through 89. The raw scores above the mean of the five highest were assigned T scores in equal intervals from 90 through 100. The T score assigned to each raw total problem score is displayed in a box to the right of the hand-scored profile and is printed out by the computer-scoring program.

NORMAL, BORDERLINE, AND CLINICAL RANGES

Syndrome Scales

As shown in Figure 3-1, broken lines are printed across the profile at the T scores of 67 and 70. These represent a borderline clinical range in which scores are not so clearly in the clinical range as those that are above $T = 70$. The borderline range was chosen to provide efficient discrimination between demographically matched referred and nonreferred samples (described in Chapter 6), while minimizing the number of "false positives," i.e., normal children who score in the clinical range. If maximum discrimination is sought between deviant and nondeviant children without regard to the increase in false positives, cutpoints below $T = 67$ on the syndrome scales may improve discrimination in some samples.

There is no well-validated criterion for categorically distinguishing between children who are "normal" and those who are "abnormal" with respect to each syndrome. Because children are continually changing and because all assessment procedures are subject to errors of measurement and other limitations, no single score precisely indicates a child's status. Instead, a child's score on a syndrome scale should be considered an approximation of the child's status as seen by a particular informant at the time the informant completes the TRF.

The test-retest reliability of teachers' ratings is high (Chapter 5) and the standard error of measurement is small (Appendix B). This means that, on the average, the range of scores represented by a particular score is relatively narrow. Nevertheless, in deciding whether a child is clinically deviant on a particular syndrome, it is important to remember that each score is just one point on a continuum of quantitative variation. It is especially important to be aware of such variation when a score is at the low end of the clinical range. When a syndrome score is on or between the broken lines, it should be described as "borderline clinical."

If a specific categorical cutpoint is desired for statistical purposes, the *T* score of 67 can be used to represent the bottom of the clinical range. As shown in Chapter 6, cutpoints at *T* scores of 67 significantly discriminated between referred and nonreferred children on the eight cross-informant syndromes scored from the TRF. Furthermore, there were significant differences between the proportions of referred and nonreferred children scoring in the normal, borderline, and clinical ranges. These findings support the cutpoint of *T* = 67 and the tripartite division into the normal, borderline, and clinical ranges. However, other cutpoints and borderline ranges might be chosen for particular research objectives with particular samples.

Total Problem Score

To test the discriminative efficiency of various cutpoints, we used a Relative Operating Characteristics (ROC) type of analysis (Swets & Pickett, 1982). We did this by comparing the distributions of total problem scores in demographically matched referred and nonreferred children, separately for each sex in each of the two age ranges. (The matched samples are described in Chapter 6). For each sex/age group, we identified a range of scores where the differences between the cumulative percents of referred and nonreferred children were greatest. That is, we computed the difference between the cumulative percent of referred children who obtained all scores up to a particular score and the cumulative percent of nonreferred children who obtained all scores up to that same score. The score at which the nonreferred children exceeded the referred children by the greatest percent represented the most efficient cutpoint, in terms of minimizing the percent of nonreferred children who scored above the cutpoint ("false positives"), *plus* the percent of referred children who scored *below* the cutpoint ("false negatives").

The cutpoints for both sexes and all age ranges on the TRF, CBCL, and YSR, were compared to determine whether a similar cutpoint and borderline range could provide efficient discrimination for all of them. Scores in the normative samples ranging from about the 82nd to the 90th percentile were found to provide the most efficient discrimination for most sex/age groups on all three instruments. T scores of 60 to 63, which span these percentiles, were therefore chosen to demarcate the borderline clinical range.

For categorical discrimination between deviant and nondeviant groups, $T = 60$ serves as the bottom of the clinical range. However, by designating a borderline clinical range, we emphasize that T scores from 60 to 63 are less clearly deviant than scores above it. Furthermore, cutpoints other than $T = 60$ may be more effective for particular purposes in particular samples.

SUMMARY

Beside describing children in terms of specific items, the TRF is designed to identify syndromes of problems. To identify syndromes, we performed principal components/ varimax analyses of the TRF problem items scored for clinically referred children, separately for each sex at ages 5-11 and 12-18. Two sets of analyses were performed for each sex/age group. In one set of analyses, all but the very low prevalence problem items were included. In the second set, only the 89 items common to the TRF, CBCL, and YSR were included.

Syndromes identified in multiple sex/age groups were compared to identify items that were common to a syndrome across sex/age groups. These items were used to construct a *core syndrome* of items to be scored on the 1991 TRF profile. The version of the core syndrome derived from the 89 common items was compared with analogous core syndromes derived from the CBCL and YSR. Items that were found in the analogous core syndrome from at least two of the three instruments were used to form a *cross-informant syndrome construct*.

The following eight cross-informant syndromes are displayed on the 1991 TRF profile: *Withdrawn, Somatic Complaints, Anxious/Depressed, Social Problems, Thought Problems, Attention Problems, Delinquent Behavior,* and *Aggressive Behavior*.

Profiles for hand scoring and computer scoring the TRF display scores for every problem item, as well as raw scores and *T* scores for the syndrome scales, Internalizing, Externalizing, and total problem score. Normal, borderline, and clinical ranges are also designated for the scale scores.

Chapter 4
Internalizing and Externalizing
Groupings of Syndromes

As shown in Figure 3-1, the syndrome scales designated as *Withdrawn, Somatic Complaints*, and *Anxious/Depressed* are grouped under the heading *Internalizing*. The syndrome scales designated as *Delinquent Behavior* and *Aggressive Behavior* are grouped under the heading *Externalizing*. These groupings of syndromes reflect a distinction that has been detected in numerous multivariate analyses of children's behavioral/ emotional problems. The two groups of problems have been variously called Personality Problem versus Conduct Problem (Peterson, 1961), Internalizing versus Externalizing (Achenbach, 1966), Inhibition versus Aggression (Miller, 1967), and Overcontrolled versus Undercontrolled (Achenbach & Edelbrock, 1978).

In the pre-1991 profiles, we identified two broad groupings of syndromes that we designated as Internalizing and Externalizing, consistent with the terminology used since the initial multivariate study in this research program (Achenbach, 1966). The pre-1991 groupings were identified by performing second-order principal components analyses of the syndrome scales for each sex/age group on the TRF, CBCL, and YSR. Each group's Internalizing and Externalizing scores were based on their respective set of syndromes. Because the syndrome scales and the items of these scales varied somewhat from one sex/age group and instrument to another, the composition of the Internalizing and Externalizing scores was not uniform.

1991 INTERNALIZING AND
EXTERNALIZING GROUPINGS

To increase the consistency between the different sex/age groups on the TRF, CBCL, and YSR and between these instruments, we derived the 1991 Internalizing and Externalizing groupings as follows:

1. Using the clinical samples from which our syndrome scales were derived, we computed correlations between the raw scores on the syndrome scales separately for each sex/age group on the TRF, CBCL, and YSR. Items that appear on more than one scale were scored only on the scale for which they had the highest loading.

2. We performed principal factor analyses of the correlations among the scale scores separately for each sex/age group. Principal factor analyses are like principal components analyses except that estimates of communality among the variables are used instead of 1.0 in the principal diagonal. Our choice of factor analysis here was based on new evidence for the superiority of factor analysis in applications to small numbers of variables, such as our eight syndrome scales (Snook & Gorsuch, 1989). Squared multiple correlations among syndrome scale scores were used in the principal diagonal.

3. The two largest factors in each solution were rotated to the varimax criterion. Both rotated factors had eigenvalues >1.0 in all groups.

4. Averaged across all groups on all three instruments, the loadings of the syndrome scales yielded the following rank order of syndromes on the Internalizing factors (mean loadings are in parentheses): 1. Withdrawn (.784); 2. Somatic Complaints (.690); 3. Anxious/

Depressed (.650). The rank order of syndromes on the Externalizing factors was: 1. Aggressive Behavior (.791); 2. Delinquent Behavior (.778).

5. The Internalizing score for each profile is the sum of items on the three Internalizing scales of that profile. The Externalizing score is the sum of items on the two Externalizing scales of that profile. No item is counted twice within either the Internalizing score or the Externalizing score, and no item is included in both an Internalizing and Externalizing scale.

6. Because the composition of some syndrome scales differs among the profiles, there are small differences among the TRF, CBCL, and YSR versions of the Internalizing and Externalizing scores.

Although the Attention Problems scale had moderately high loadings on the various versions of the Externalizing factor, its mean loading of .618 was enough lower than the mean loading of .791 for the Aggressive scale and .778 for the Delinquent scale that it was deemed inappropriate to include with the Externalizing grouping. The Attention Problems scale is therefore displayed in the middle section of the profiles with the Social Problems and Thought Problems scales, neither of which had consistently high loadings on the Internalizing or Externalizing factors.

Starting on the left side of the profile, the Internalizing scales are listed from left to right in descending order of their rank on the Internalizing factors (Withdrawn, Somatic Complaints, Anxious/Depressed). On the right side of the profile, the two Externalizing scales are listed from left to right in ascending order of their rank on the Externalizing factors, i. e., Delinquent Behavior, followed by Aggressive Behavior, which is the rightmost scale.

ASSIGNMENT OF INTERNALIZING AND EXTERNALIZING T SCORES

To provide norm referenced scores, we summed the scores obtained on the Internalizing and Externalizing items by the normative samples of each sex/age group on each instrument. The one item that appears on more than one Internalizing scale was counted only once in the Internalizing score. No items of the Delinquent or Aggressive Behavior scales are included on any other syndrome scale.

Percentiles were computed according to the procedure described in Chapter 2. Normalized T scores were assigned in the same manner as described in Chapter 3 for the total problem scores. That is, the T scores were based directly on percentiles up to the 97.7th percentile ($T = 70$). The raw scores ranging from $T = 70$ to the mean of the five highest scores in our clinical samples were then assigned T scores in equal intervals from 71 through 89. The raw scores above the mean of the five highest in our clinical samples were assigned T scores in equal intervals from 90 through 100. Just as with the total problem score, the clinical cutpoint was established at $T = 60$, with the borderline clinical range including T scores of 60 through 63.

To assess a child's problems in terms of the Internalizing and Externalizing groupings, the hand-scored profiles provide guidelines for summing the Internalizing and Externalizing scale scores. Appendix A provides detailed scoring instructions. (Although one item is included on more than one Internalizing scale, this item is counted only once in computing the Internalizing score.) To the right of the profile, a table is provided for determining the T score equivalent of each Internalizing and Externalizing raw score (see Appendix A for instructions). The computer-scoring programs automatically compute raw scores and T scores for Internalizing and Externalizing.

RELATIONS BETWEEN INTERNALIZING
AND EXTERNALIZING SCORES

The Internalizing and Externalizing groupings reflect empirical associations among subsets of scales that involve contrasting kinds of problems. These problems are not mutually exclusive, however, because some individuals may have both kinds of problems. In many samples of children, positive correlations are found between Internalizing and Externalizing scores. Across our normative samples of each sex/age group on each instrument, the mean correlation between Internalizing and Externalizing was .52, computed by Fisher's z transformation. This reflects the fact that children who have very high problem scores in one of the two areas also tend to have at least above-average problem scores in the other area as well. Conversely, children who have very low scores in one area also tend to have relatively low scores in the other area.

Appendix C lists the correlations between TRF Internalizing and Externalizing scores for demographically matched referred and nonreferred samples of each sex in each age range. The mean Pearson r between TRF Internalizing and Externalizing scores was .35 for the referred samples and .41 for the non-referred samples, computed by z transformation.

Despite the positive association between Internalizing and Externalizing scores found in our samples as a whole, some children's problems are primarily Internalizing, whereas other children's problems are primarily Externalizing. This is analogous to the relation between Verbal IQ and Performance IQ on the Wechsler intelligence tests: In most samples of children, there is a positive correlation between the Wechsler Verbal IQ and Performance IQ (e.g., Wechsler, 1989). Nevertheless, some children have much higher Verbal than Performance scores or vice versa. Children who have much higher Verbal than Performance scores may differ in other important ways from children who have much higher Performance than Verbal scores. Similarly, children who have much higher Internalizing scores than Externalizing scores may differ in other important ways from those who show the opposite pattern. Numerous studies have in fact shown significant differences between children classified as having primarily Internalizing versus primarily Externalizing problems (e.g., Achenbach, 1966; Achenbach & Lewis, 1971; Katz, Zigler, & Zalk, 1975; McConaughy, Achenbach, & Gent, 1988; Weintraub, 1973).

Distinguishing Between Internalizing and Externalizing Patterns

Users of the profiles may wish to distinguish between children whose reported problems are primarily from the Internalizing grouping and those whose problems are primarily from the Externalizing grouping. Such distinctions may be clinically useful for choosing approaches to intervention and for identifying groups of pupils with similar problems for purposes such as types of special education. Such distinctions may also be useful for testing hypotheses about differences in etiology, responsiveness to particular interventions, and long-term outcomes.

The specific criteria for distinguishing between children having primarily Internalizing versus Externalizing problems should be based on the user's aims and the size and nature of the available sample. The criteria chosen for distinguishing between Internalizing and Externalizing patterns will affect the proportion of a sample that can be classified, the homogeneity of the resulting groups, and the associations that may be found between the Internalizing-Externalizing classification and other variables. Very stringent criteria, for example, will severely limit the proportion of children classified as manifesting Internalizing versus Externalizing patterns. But stringent criteria will also yield relatively extreme groups who are likely to differ more on other variables than would less extreme Internalizing and Externalizing groups.

The trade-offs between stringency of criteria, proportion of children classified, and degree of association with other variables must be weighed by users of the profiles when choosing criteria for their own purposes. As a general guideline, we suggest that children not be classified as Internalizing or Externalizing unless *(a)* their total problem score exceeds the clinical cutoff on at least one of the three instruments, and *(b)* the difference between their Internalizing and Externalizing *T* score is at least 10 points on one instrument *or* at least 5 points on two instruments. The larger the difference is between *T* scores and the more consistent the difference is between two or more instruments, the more distinctive the Internalizing and Externalizing groups will be.

SUMMARY

Internalizing and Externalizing groupings of behavioral/emotional problems were identified by performing second-order factor analyses of the eight 1991 syndrome scales scored separately from each instrument for each sex/age group. The largest two rotated factors in all analyses reflected a distinction between problems of withdrawal, somatic complaints, and anxiety/depression, on the one hand, and delinquent and aggressive behavior, on the other.

On all 1991 profiles, the Internalizing grouping is operationally defined as the sum of scores on the problem items of the Withdrawan, Somatic Complaints, and Anxious/ Depressed scales. The Externalizing grouping is defined as the sum of scores on the problem items of the Delinquent and Aggressive Behavior scales.

The eight scales of the profiles are arranged in order starting with the three Internalizing scales on the left, followed by three scales that did not have consistently high loadings on either the Internalizing or Externalizing factors (Social Problems, Thought Problems, Attention Problems), and ending with the two Externalizing scales on the right. *T* scores were assigned to the Internalizing and Externalizing scores in the same way as was done for the total problem scores.

The relations between Internalizing and Externalizing scores is analogous to the relation between verbal and performance IQ scores on intelligence tests. Although Internalizing and Externalizing scores represent contrasting kinds of problems, they are not mutually exclusive. Across groups of children, Internalizing scores typically correlate positively with Externalizing scores, because children who have very high scores in one area tend to have at least above-average scores in the other area as well. Nevertheless, children who have much higher Internalizing than Externalizing scores may differ in important ways from children who show the reverse pattern. Guidelines were provided for distinguishing between children whose problems are primarily in the Internalizing area and those whose problems are primarily in the Externalizing area.

Chapter 5
Reliability, Stability, and
Inter-Teacher Agreement

Reliability refers to agreement between repeated assessments of phenomena when the phenomena themselves remain constant. When rating instruments such as the TRF are self-administered, it is important to know the degree to which the same informants provide the same scores over periods when the subjects' behavior is not expected to change, i.e., the degree of *test-retest reliability*. This chapter presents test-retest reliability obtained when teachers independently completed TRFs at a mean interval of 15 days.

Beside reliability, it is also helpful to know the degree of stability in scores over periods long enough that pupils' behavior may change and also the degree of agreement between scores from different teachers. Long-term stability and inter-teacher agreement are not expected to be as high as test-retest reliability, because reliability involves agreement between assessments of the *same* phenomena. The same teachers rerating behavior over long periods are likely to see different behaviors at different times. Analogously, different teachers are apt to observe different samples of pupils' behavior. Findings for stability and inter-teacher agreement are therefore presented separately from findings for reliability.

An additional property of scales is their *internal consistency*. This refers to the correlation between half of a scale's items and the other half of its items. Although internal consistency is sometimes referred to as "split-half reliability," it cannot tell us the degree to which a scale will produce the same results over different occasions when the target phenomena are expected to remain constant. Furthermore, scales with relatively low internal consistency may be more *valid* than scales with very high internal consistency. For example, if a scale consists of 20 repetitions of exactly the same item, it should produce very high internal consistency, because respondents should repeatedly score the same item the same way on a particular occasion. However, such a scale would usually be less valid than a scale that uses 20 different items to assess the same phenomenon. Because each of the 20 different items is likely to tap different aspects of the target phenomenon and to be subject to different errors of measurement, the 20 different items are likely to provide better measurement despite lower internal consistency than a scale that repeats the same item 20 times.

Our syndrome scales were derived from principal components analyses of the correlations among items. The composition of the scales is therefore based on internal consistency among certain subsets of items. Measures of the internal consistency of these scales are thus redundant. Nevertheless, because some users may wish to know the degree of internal consistency of our scales, Cronbach's (1951) *alpha* is displayed for each problem scale in Appendix B. *Alpha* represents the mean of the correlations between all possible sets of half the items comprising a scale. *Alpha* tends to be directly related to the length of the scale, because half the items of a short scale provide a less stable measure than half the items of a long scale.

TEST-RETEST RELIABILITY OF SCORES

To assess reliability in both the rank ordering and magnitude of scale scores, we computed test-retest correlations and *t* tests of differences between teachers' ratings of 44 8- and 9-year-old pupils at a mean interval of 15 days (range = 7 to 30 days). Most of the pupils had been low birthweight infants, while about one-third had been full-term infants who were participating in a longitudinal comparison with the low birthweight children (Achenbach, Phares, Howell, Rauh, & Nurcombe, 1990). They were in different classrooms of many different school systems. Their mean TRF scores were in the normal range.

Table 5-1 shows the correlations for boys and girls separately, as well as for both sexes combined. All test-retest rs were significant at $p < .01$, except Thought Problems for the girls, where nearly all scores were 0. The mean of the rs for the adaptive scales was .90, while the mean of the rs for all problem scales was .92. Four scales showed significant ($p < .05$) differences in mean scores over the 15-day interval. However, this was fewer than the seven expected by chance, using a .01 protection level (Sakoda, Cohen, & Beall, 1954).

TWO- AND FOUR-MONTH STABILITY OF PROBLEM SCORES

Table 5-2 displays correlations between TRF problem scale scores obtained at 2- and 4-month intervals by 19 boys who were referred for special services for behavioral/emotional problems. The mean correlations of .75 over 2 months and .66 over 4 months indicate good stability in scores despite the possible effects of the services received and/or the regression toward the mean that would be expected for subjects considered to be deviant. Both of these effects could also have contributed to the significant decline in nine of the scale scores (compared to five expected by chance). However, such a decline is often found in ratings and in psychiatric interviews of all kinds of samples using different kinds of informants (e.g., Achenbach, 1991b; Edelbrock, Costello, Dulcan, Kalas, & Conover, 1985; Evans, 1975; Milich, Roberts, Loney, & Caputo, 1980; Miller, Hampe, Barrett, & Noble, 1972).

Table 5-1
TRF 15-Day Test-Retest Reliabilities

Score	Boys	Girls	Combined
N =	27	17	44
Mean Academic Performance	.95	.91	.93
Working Hard	.94	.94	.93
Behaving Appropriately	.81	.86	.83
Learning	.91	.87	.90
Happy	.74	.88	.78
Total Adaptive	.93	.94	.93
Mean r	.90	.90	.90
Withdrawn	.93	.95	.93
Somatic Complaints	.82	.98	.85
Anxious/Depressed	.89	.83	.88
Social Problems	.92	.99	.96
Thought Problems	.84	(.43)	.82
Attention Problems	.95	.98	.96
Delinquent Behavior	.92	.88	.87
Aggressive Behavior	.84	.97	.91
Internalizing	.92	.87	.91
Externalizing	.86	.97	.92
Total Problems	.92	.99	.95
Mean r	.90	.95	.92

Note. All Pearson rs were significant at $p < .0001$ except the one in parentheses. There were fewer significant differences between Time 1 and Time 2 mean scores than expected by chance.

INTER-TEACHER AGREEMENT

Table 5-3 displays correlations between TRF ratings by pairs of teachers for pupils who were referred for mental health or special education services for behavioral/emotional problems. Most pairs of teachers rating the same pupil saw the pupil in different classes or under conditions that differed in other ways. The magnitude of the correlations did not differ much among the four sex/age groups, although it tended to be lowest for 12-18-year-old boys for both the adaptive and problem scores. Of the specific scores, the highest correlations were for Aggressive Behavior (r = .68 in the combined groups) and Externalizing (r = .66 in the combined groups).

Table 5-2
Two- and Four-Month Stability of TRF Problem
Scores for 19 Boys Aged 7-11

Scale	2 months	4 months
Withdrawn	.77	.66
Somatic Complaints	(.36)	.47
Anxious/Depressed	.86	.71
Social Problems	.61	(.27)
Thought Problems	.72	.88[ab]
Attention Problems	.77[ab]	.73[ab]
Delinquent Behavior	.73	.66
Aggressive Behavior	.77[a]	.68[a]
Internalizing	.89	.62
Externalizing	.77[a]	.68[ab]
Total Problems	.78[a]	.60[ab]
Mean r	.75	.66

Note. Table entries are Pearson correlations between teachers' ratings obtained at 2- and 4-month intervals for 19 boys who had been referred for special services for behavioral/emotional problems but who attended regular classes most of the school day. All correlations were significant at p <.05 except the two in parentheses.
[a]Initial score > 2- or 4-month score significant by t test at p <.05.
[b]When corrected for the number of comparisons, difference in means was not significant.

Odds Ratios for Scores in the Normal versus Clinical Range

The rightmost column of Table 5-3 displays relative risk odds ratios (Fleiss, 1981) indicating the degree of agreement

Table 5-3
Agreement Between Teachers
Rating Pupils Referred for Evaluation

| | Boys | | Girls | | | Odds |
	5-11	12-18	5-11	12-18	Combined	Ratio
N =	55	92	22	38	207	
Academic Performance	.74	.61	.66	.48	.62	10.1
Working Hard	.60	.51	.64	.54	.54	N/A
Behaving Appropriately	.48	.38	.69	.53	.47	N/A
Learning	.56	.56	.48	.47	.54	N/A
Happy	.54	.42	(.36)	.87	.53	N/A
Total Adaptive	.69	.53	.59	.66	.61	9.2
Mean r	.61	.51	.58	.62	.55	
Withdrawn	.58	.55	(-.05)	.59	.55	7.5
Somatic Complaints	.42	.37	.55	(.19)	.30	5.9
Anxious/Depressed	.53	.24	.79	(.30)	.40	3.3
Social Problems	.70	.49	.78	.52	.58	9.7
Thought Problems	.56	.59	.50	.39	.52	14.5
Attention Problems	.65	.56	.67	.55	.61	5.8
Delinquent Behavior	.44	.51	.46	.73	.56	12.9
Aggressive Behavior	.70	.61	.81	.74	.68	14.9
Internalizing	.49	.36	.50	(.30)	.41	4.5
Externalizing	.69	.59	.79	.73	.66	6.2
Total Problems	.68	.53	.65	.66	.60	6.3
Mean r	.60	.50	.62	.54	.54	

Note. All Pearson *r*s were significant at $p < .05$ except the ones in parentheses. All odds ratios were significant at $p < .01$.

between teachers in scoring pupils in the normal versus clinical range. Because odds ratios are nonparametric statistics based on 2 x 2 tables, pupils of both sexes and all ages were combined. The odds ratios in Table 5-3 indicate the elevation in odds that pupils would be scored in the clinical range by one teacher if they had been scored in the clinical range by the other teacher, as compared to the odds for pupils who had not been scored in the clinical range by their first teacher. Thus, for example, the odds ratio of 14.9 for Aggressive Behavior in Table 5-3 means that pupils scored in the clinical range by one teacher were 14.9 times more likely to be scored in the clinical range by their other teacher than were pupils who had not been scored in the clinical range by their first teacher. Confidence intervals showed that all the odds ratios were significantly greater than 1.0, at $p<.01$, demonstrating good agreement between ratings by teachers in classifying pupils in the normal versus clinical range.

Correlations Between Teachers and Teacher Aides

Table 5-4 displays correlations between TRF ratings by teachers and teacher aides for special education pupils. In this case, both types of raters were generally seeing the pupils under similar conditions, although the raters differed with respect to their training and roles. The correlations were similar in magnitude to those shown in Table 5-3 for pairs of teachers seeing pupils in different classes. As with the pairs of teachers, the correlations tended to be lowest for 12- to 18-year-old boys, and the scales showing the highest correlations were Aggressive Behavior ($r = .71$ in the combined groups) and Externalizing ($r = .69$). Externalizing behaviors in general and aggressive behaviors in particular may elicit relatively high agreement because they are especially obvious to school personnel.

All significant differences in mean scores reflected higher adaptive behavior scores and lower problem scores in ratings by aides than by teachers, as indicated by the superscripts in Table 5-4. Whether because of differences in level of training or differences in attitudes, aides' ratings thus provided a more favorable impression of special education pupils' functioning. As might be expected, the correlations for ratings of Academic Performance were lower between aides and teachers ($r = .35$ for all the pupils in Table 5-4) than between pairs of teachers ($r = .62$ for all the pupils in Table 5-3), a difference that was

Table 5-4
Teacher-Teacher Aide Agreement for
Special Education Pupils

Score		Boys		Girls		
		5-11	12-18	5-11	12-18	Combined
	$N =$	320	111	147	57	635
Academic Performance		$.23^a$	$.44^{ac}$	.34	.67	$.35^a$
Working Hard		.70	.60	.66	.82	.69
Behaving Appropriately		.62	.49	.64	.84	.66
Learning		.60	$.44^{ac}$	.57	.77	$.58^{ac}$
Happy		.57	.57	.56	.74	.59
Total Adaptive		.64	.56	.63	.82	.65
Mean r		.57	.52	.57	.78	.60
Withdrawn		$.49^b$	.51	.43	.31	$.46^b$
Somatic Complaints		.65	.20	.39	.27	$.46^{bc}$
Anxious/Depressed		$.50^{bc}$	.42	$.42^{bc}$	.42	$.46^b$
Social Problems		$.61^b$	.44	$.58^{bc}$	$.69^{bc}$	$.58^b$
Thought Problems		.44	.27	.24	.27	.38
Attention Problems		$.62^b$	.60	.49	.69	$.62^b$
Delinquent Behavior		$.55^b$	.44	.55	.57	$.55^b$
Aggressive Behavior		$.72^b$	.58	.73	.59	$.71^b$
Internalizing		$.48^{bc}$	.41	$.43^{bc}$	.27	$.44^b$
Externalizing		$.70^b$	.57	.72	.60	$.69^b$
Total Problems		$.60^b$	.47	.52	.53	$.57^b$
Mean r		.59	.45	.51	.49	.55

Note. Table entries are Pearson correlations between teachers and teacher aides for pupils in special education classes. All correlations were significant at $p < .05$.
[a]Teacher < teacher aide, $p < .05$, by t test.
[b]Teacher > teacher aide, $p < .05$, by t test.
[c]Not significant when corrected for number of comparisons.

significant at $p < .001$). The moderate levels of inter-teacher and teacher-teacher aide agreement underscore the importance of obtaining TRFs from multiple informants when possible.

SUMMARY

The test-retest reliability of the TRF was found to be high over a mean interval of 15 days, with the mean $r = .90$ for academic and adaptive scores and .92 for problem scores. Stability was good over 2- and 4-month periods. Inter-rater agreement was similar for teachers seeing pupils under different conditions (mean $r = .55$ for academic and adaptive scores; $r = .54$ for problem scores), and for teachers versus teacher aides seeing pupils under more similar conditions ($r = .60$ for academic and adaptive scores; $r = .55$ for problem scores).

Chapter 6
Validity

Validity concerns the accuracy with which a procedure measures what it is supposed to measure. The TRF is designed to obtain teachers' reports of their pupils' problems and adaptive functioning in a standardized format. As with most procedures for assessing behavioral/emotional problems, the TRF must be evaluated in relation to a variety of criteria, none of which is definitive by itself. We will consider findings on the TRF with respect to *content validity, construct validity,* and *criterion-related validity.*

CONTENT VALIDITY

Content validity refers to whether an instrument's content includes what it is intended to measure. The problem items of the TRF were designed to tap the same problems as the CBCL, with the exception of those that teachers were not expect to know about. As detailed in Chapter 1 of the CBCL *Manual* (Achenbach, 1991a), the CBCL items are descriptions of competencies and problems that are of concern to parents and mental health workers. The descriptions were derived from earlier research (Achenbach, 1966), the clinical and research literature, and consultation with clinical and developmental psychologists, psychiatrists, and social workers. Pilot editions of the CBCL were tested with parents in several clinics. Successive revisions were made on the basis of feedback from parents, paraprofessionals, and clinicians. After finalizing the CBCL items, we compared scores obtained by 1,300 children referred for mental health services and 1,300 demographically similar nonreferred children (Achenbach & Edelbrock, 1981).

On all but two of the CBCL problem items (*Allergy* and *Asthma*), referred children scored significantly higher than nonreferred children ($p < .005$). These findings showed that, with the exception of the two nonsignificant items, the CBCL problem items were associated with judgments of children's need for mental health services. The CBCL findings were replicated in our 1989 national sample. Because Allergy and Asthma again failed to discriminate significantly between referred and nonreferred samples on either the CBCL or the YSR, these items are not counted in the total problem scores for either of those instruments (these items do not appear on the TRF).

Although many of the TRF problem items were taken directly from the CBCL, some were modified slightly to make them more appropriate for teachers. Twenty-five of the CBCL items were replaced with items that were more appropriate for teachers. The replacement items, which are marked with superscript *a* in Figure 1-2, were developed from reviews of other teacher rating forms and pilot testing in schools to obtain items that teachers would be able to judge. The academic performance and adaptive functioning items of the TRF were similarly chosen to obtain judgments that teachers are especially able to make with respect to children's functioning in school.

To test the association of teachers' ratings of TRF items with referral for mental health or special education services, we compared the scores obtained on every item by 1,275 pupils referred for services for behavioral/emotional problems and 1,275 demographically similar nonreferred pupils drawn from the 1989 normative sample described in Chapter 2. The nonreferred and referred samples were precisely matched for sex and age and were matched as closely as possible for SES and ethnicity. On Hollingshead's (1975) 9-step scale for parental occupation, the mean SES was 5.7 (SD = 2.1) for the nonreferred sample and 5.3 (SD = 2.7) for the referred sample.

Ethnicity was 77% white, 14% black, and 9% mixed or other for the nonreferred sample, compared to 76% white, 18% black, and 7% mixed or other for the referred sample.

As detailed in Chapter 7, the referred pupils obtained significantly higher scores on nearly all the TRF problem items and lower scores on all the adaptive functioning items than the nonreferred pupils. This demonstrates that the TRF items indeed related to mental health concerns. However, prospective users should judge whether the content of the TRF items is suitable for their particular purposes.

CONSTRUCT VALIDITY

Construct validity concerns the assessment of hypothesized variables (*hypothetical constructs*) for which there is no definitive criterion measure. A primary reason for developing the TRF, CBCL, and YSR was to identify problems that tend to co-occur, because there was little previous basis for identifying and distinguishing among childhood disorders. The empirical derivation of syndromes of co-occurring problems was detailed in Chapter 3. The eight cross-informant syndromes scorable from the TRF, CBCL, and YSR provide common foci for assessing children from the perspectives of teacher-, parent-, and self-reports. As discussed in Chapter 3, the cross-informant syndromes represent constructs or "latent variables" in the sense of hypothetical variables that may not be perfectly measured by any single procedure. Teacher-, parent-, and self-reports, plus other data, may all be relevant to assessing differences among children with respect to the cross-informant syndrome constructs. The "construct validity" of constructs such as these syndromes involves a "nomological network" of interrelated procedures to reflect the hypothesized variables in different ways (Cronbach & Meehl, 1955).

A key index of the validity of the syndrome scores is their ability to identify children whose problems arouse enough concern to warrant referral for professional help, as will be addressed in the section on criterion-related validity. Successful applications of the scales for a variety of assessment tasks progressively build confidence in their construct validity. Such applications have been reported in over 100 published studies of the pre-1991 TRF scales (Achenbach & Brown, 1991, list the studies). Because most of the 1991 TRF scales correlate very highly with the pre-1991 scales (as shown in Table 8-1), the findings are generally applicable to the 1991 scales, as well.

Among the few other teacher rating scales that assess empirically derived syndromes, the Conners Revised Teacher Rating Scale (Goyette, Conners, & Ulrich, 1978) is probably the most widely used. Although the Conners Scale is designed primarily for assessing hyperactivity, it does provide a test of construct validity with respect to those of its scales that have counterparts on the TRF. Table 6-1 displays Pearson correlations between TRF scores and Conners scores for children who were referred for mental health or special education services. For each child, the TRF and the Conners were completed by the child's teacher, with an average interval of 6.8 days between the two instruments.

The boxes in Table 6-1 indicate correlations between the TRF and Conners scales that are most similar to one another. As Table 6-1 shows, TRF scales correlated from .80 to .83 with the Conners Conduct Problems, Inattention-Passivity, and total problem scores. The closest counterparts of the Conners Hyperactivity scale were the TRF Aggressive Behavior ($r = .67$) and Externalizing ($r = .63$) scales, while the closest counterpart of the Conners Hyperactivity Index was the TRF total problems score ($r = .71$). Although the Conners scale is not designed to tap Internalizing problems and the TRF does not have a hyperactivity scale separate from the Attention Problems scale, the relations between the counterpart TRF and Conners scales are as strong as those found between different tests of cognitive abilities (e.g., Wechsler, 1989).

Table 6-1
Pearson Correlations Between TRF Scores
and Conners Revised Teacher Rating Scale

			Conners		
TRF	*Conduct Problem*	*Hyper-activity*	*Inatt.-Passiv.*	*Hyper-activity Index*	*Total Probs*
Academic Performance	(.06)	(-.09)	-.34	(-.12)	(-.10)
Working Hard	(-.24)	(-.20)	-.56	-.40	-.37
Behaving Appropriately	-.48	-.66	-.39	-.62	-.67
Learning	-.31	-.36	-.63	-.51	-.49
Happy	-.68	-.31	-.35	-.49	-.61
Total Adaptive	-.59	-.51	-.66	-.68	-.71
Withdrawn	.34	(-.11)	.43	(.14)	.30
Somatic Complaints	(.03)	(.10)	.43	(.18)	(.25)
Anxious/Depressed	.41	(.08)	.32	(.22)	.38
Social Problems	.60	(.25)	.51	.45	.63
Thought Problems	(.10)	(.19)	(.20)	(.26)	(.21)
Attention Problems	.34	.41	⟦.80⟧	.60	.63
Delinquent Behavior	.62	(.22)	(.25)	.38	.53
Aggressive Behavior	⟦.80⟧	⟦.67⟧	(.14)	.69	.74
Internalizing	.39	(.02)	.42	(.21)	.38
Externalizing	⟦.83⟧	⟦.63⟧	(.18)	.68	.76
Total Problems	.76	.52	.58	⟦.71⟧	⟦.83⟧

Note. Pearson *r*s between TRF scores and Conners Revised Teacher Rating Scale (Goyette, Conners, & Ulrich, 1978) completed at a mean interval of 6.8 days. $N = 38$ boys and 7 girls aged 5-16. All *r*s were significant at $p < .05$ except those in parentheses. Boxes indicate *r*s between the most similar scales on the two instruments.

Other evidence of construct validity comes from studies of the TRF scores of pupils who differed in diagnoses made independently of the TRF. In one study, Edelbrock, Costello, and Kessler (1984) found that children diagnosed as having attention deficit disorders (ADD) scored significantly higher on the pre-1991 TRF Inattentive scale than a control group of referred children having other diagnoses. Those diagnosed as ADD with hyperactivity scored significantly lower than those diagnosed ADD without hyperactivity on the Social Withdrawal scale, but significantly higher on several other scales. (Table 8-1 shows the correlations between pre-1991 and 1991 TRF scales.) In another study, Harris, King, Reifler, and Rosenberg (1984) found that special education pupils diagnosed as having emotional disorders were significantly more deviant on the TRF problem scales than special education pupils diagnosed as having learning disorders. TRF scores have also been found to correlate significantly with ratings of school behavior made by classroom observers who were blind to the TRF scores (Reed & Edelbrock, 1983) and to discriminate significantly among referred children differing in CBCL profile patterns (McConaughy, Achenbach, & Gent, 1988).

CRITERION-RELATED VALIDITY

As done with the CBCL and YSR, we used referral for services for behavioral/emotional problems as a general criterion against which to test the discriminative power of the TRF scales. Because Public Law 94-142 (Education of the Handicapped Act, 1977) mandates special education services for children identified as severely emotionally disturbed (SED), children receiving such services, as well as children receiving mental health services outside of school, were included in our referred criterion group. Conversely, children known to have received either special education or mental health services within the preceding year were excluded from our nonreferred criterion group. The samples consisted of the 2,550 demographically matched referred and nonreferred pupils described at the beginning of the chapter.

Referral for either special education or mental health services does not provide an infallible criterion of school children's need for help. If we were able to exclude (a) referred children who should not have been referred and (b) nonreferred children who should have been referred, this could increase the differences between scores for our referred versus nonreferred samples. Furthermore, the criterion of referral is not specific to any one of our scales. Although some children may have problems mainly of the sort included on one of our syndrome scales, other referred children may not be deviant on that scale at all but have problems in other areas.

Because the criterion of referral is fallible and referred children may be deviant in ways very different from what is represented by a particular scale, our findings may underestimate the associations between our scales and deviance specific to the area tapped by a particular scale. Nevertheless, because of the lack of other well-established validity criteria, referral for mental health or special education services seemed an ecologically more valid criterion than others that might be feasible with large representative samples (Achenbach & Edelbrock, 1981, have reviewed alternative criteria).

By comparing demographically matched referred and nonreferred samples, we prevented possible demographic differences in scores from being confounded with referral status. To assess the effects of referral status and the demographic variables, we computed multiple regressions of scale scores on referral status (scored 0 for nonreferred, 1 for referred), age, SES (Hollingshead, 1975, 9-step scale for parental occupation), and ethnicity, which was analyzed via dummy variables coded as white = 1, nonwhite = 0, and black = 1, nonblack = 0. There were not enough subjects of any one other ethnic group to warrant entry as a separate independent variable.

To take account of possible chance effects occurring in these analyses, we have marked (superscript e) the number of nominally significant effects that could have arisen by chance in the analyses of each independent variable within each sex/age group. In view of our large Ns, we used a .01 *alpha* level and a .01 protection level for determining the number of significant findings apt to occur by chance (Sakoda et al., 1954). The effects marked with superscript e are the nominally significant effects that had the smallest F values, which are assumed to be the effects most likely to be significant by chance.

Table 6-2 shows the effect size for each variable in terms of the semipartial r^2 obtained after partialling out any other independent variables that accounted for more variance in the scale score. According to Cohen's (1988) criteria for effect sizes when other independent variables are partialled out via multiple regression, effects accounting for 2 to 13% of variance in the dependent variable are considered small; effects accounting for 13 to 26% of variance are medium; and effects accounting for >26% of variance are large.

Referral Status Differences Between Scale Scores

As shown in Table 6-2, all effects of referral status that were significant at p <.01 reflected higher academic and adaptive and lower problem scores for nonreferred than referred pupils. The one effect of referral status that did not reach p <.01 approached significance (p = .066), reflecting lower scores for nonreferred than referred 12-18-year-old boys on the Somatic Complaints scale.

Referral status showed its largest effects on scores for 12- to 18-year-old girls, where 7 of the 17 analyses revealed differences between referred and nonreferred girls that met Cohen's criterion for large effects. The largest effects were on Academic Performance (30% of variance), learning (33%), happy (31%), total adaptive (36%), and total problems (32%). Three comparisons in other sex/age groups also showed effects of referral status that were large according to Cohen's criterion. Most of the other differences between referred and nonreferred pupils were in the range defined by Cohen as medium, ranging from 13 to 26% of variance.

The only scale that consistently showed small effects of referral status in all four sex/age groups was Somatic Complaints, where the effects ranged from 0.7% (p = .066) among

Table 6-2

Percent of Variance Accounted for by Significant (p <.01) Effects of Referral Status, SES, and Ethnicity in TRF Scores for Matched Referred and Nonreferred Samples

Score	668 Boys 5-11		758 Boys 12-18		518 Girls 5-11				606 Girls 12-18	
	Ref Stat[a]	SES[b]	Ref Stat[a]	SES[b]	Ref Stat[a]	SES[b]	White[c]	Black[d]	Ref Stat[a]	SES[b]
Academic Performance	21	10	19	6	22	9	--	2[N]	30	7
Working Hard	10[e]	3	11[e]	--	16	5	--	2[Ne]	25	4
Behaving Appropriately	21	2	23	2	21	--	--	2[Ne]	26	2
Learning	16	5	19	2	24	6	1[We]	--	33	6
Happy	24	3	21	2[e]	24	1	--	--	31	2
Total Adaptive	23	4	23	2	27	4	1[We]	--	36	4
Withdrawn	12	--	11[e]	3	8[e]	2	--	--	15	1[e]
Somatic Complaints	1[e]	--	--	2[e]	2[e]	--	--	--	9[e]	--
Anxious/Depressed	14	1[e]	18	--	13	--	--	--	21	--
Social Problems	28	1[e]	18	3	22	--	--	--	25	--
Thought Problems	13	--	13	--	13	1[e]	--	--	9[e]	--
Attention Problems	22	2	15	2	24	4	--	--	29	1
Delinquent Behavior	15	4	19	2	11	2	--	--	25	3
Aggressive Behavior	22	1[e]	19	2	17	--	2[N]	--	20	--
Internalizing	15	--	17	2	12	1[e]	--	--	22	--
Externalizing	22	2	20	2	17	<1	--	3[B]	23	1[e]
Total Problems	29	2	24	3	24	3	--	--	32	2

Note. Analyses were regressions of raw scores on referral status, age, SES, white vs. nonwhite, and black vs. nonblack. Variance accounted for by each independent variable is represented by the semipartial r^2 for that variable after partialling out the effects of variables accounting for more variance. Age effects did not exceed chance for any group. White-nonwhite and black-nonblack ethnicity are omitted for the three groups in which their effects did not exceed chance. [a]All adaptive scores were higher and problem scores were lower for nonreferred than referred pupils. [b]All significant SES effects reflected higher adaptive and lower problem scores for upper than lower SES pupils. [c]W = whites scored higher; N = nonwhites scored higher. [d]B = blacks scored higher; N = nonblacks scored higher. [e]Not significant when corrected for number of analyses.

12- to 18-year-old boys, to 9% among 12-18-year-old girls. These relatively weak relations no doubt reflect the fact that teachers' reports are understandably less sensitive to somatic complaints than are parent- or self-reports. Nevertheless, within certain groups, such as adolescent girls, teachers' reports of Somatic Complaints were fairly strongly associated with referral status. Beside our own evidence for criterion-related validity, other research has supported the TRF's validity in relation to independent measures of academic achievement and adjustment in the classroom (Hoge & McKay, 1986).

Demographic Differences Between Scale Scores

Age differences are not displayed in Table 6-2, because they did not exceed the number expected by chance in any of the four sex/age groups. There were no significant age differences among 5-11-year-old boys or 12-18-year-old girls, one nominally significant age difference among 5-11-year-old girls, and two among 12-18-year-old boys. Ethnic differences were also minimal, with only 5-11-year-old girls manifesting enough to exceed chance expectations. Even the ethnic differences among 5-11-year-old girls were very small, however, with the largest accounting for 3% of the variance in Externalizing scores, where blacks scored higher than non-blacks.

SES differences were more numerous, with all significant SES effects reflecting higher academic and adaptive scores and lower problem scores for upper SES than for lower SES pupils. In all four sex/age groups, the largest SES effects were on Academic Performance, ranging from 6% for 12-18-year-old boys to 10% for 5-11-year-old boys. The SES differences were much smaller on the problem scales, with no SES effects accounting for >4% of variance. Figure 6-1 displays mean scale scores for referred and nonreferred pupils of each sex for ages 5-18.

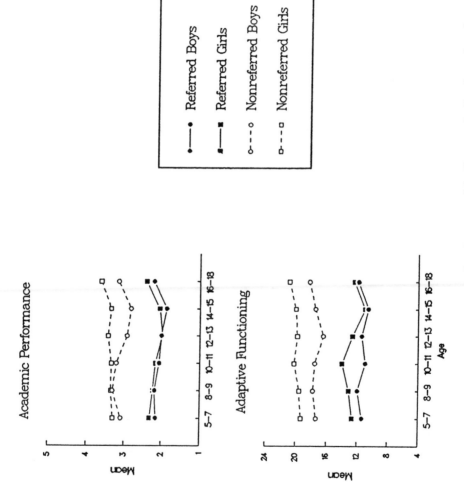

Figure 6-1. Mean TRF scale scores for demographically matched referred and nonreferred samples that were used in regression analyses.

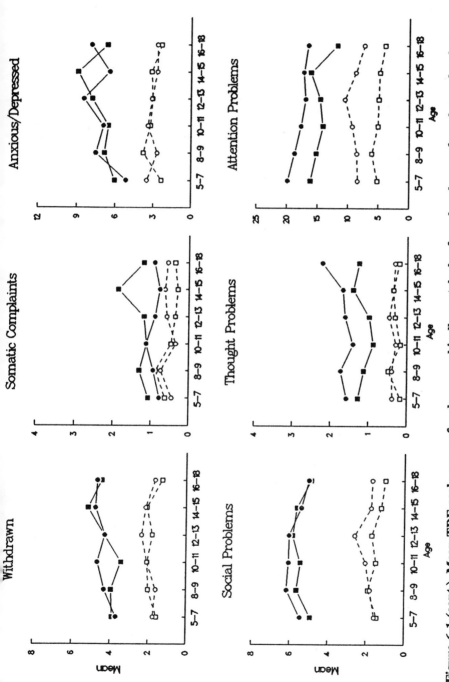

Figure 6-1 (cont). Mean TRF scale scores for demographically matched referred and nonreferred samples that were used in regression analyses.

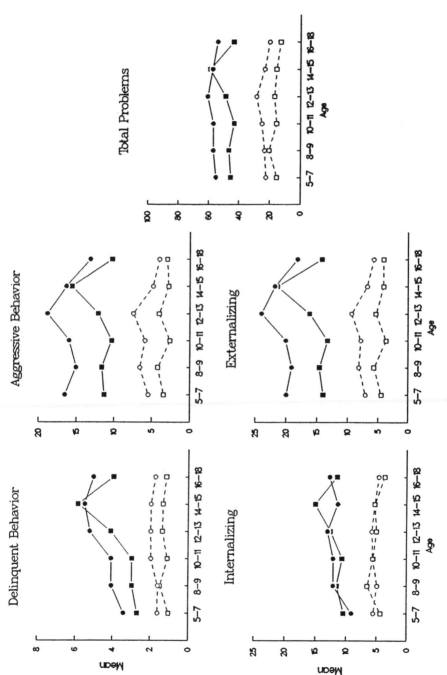

Figure 6-1 (cont.). Mean TRF scale scores for demographically matched referred and nonreferred samples that were used in regression analyses.

CLASSIFICATION OF PUPILS
ACCORDING TO CLINICAL CUTPOINTS

The regression analyses reported in the previous section showed that all but one of the TRF scales significantly discriminated between referred and nonreferred pupils with the effects of demographic variables partialled out. The Academic Performance, total adaptive, and all the problem scales have cutpoints for distinguishing categorically between the normal and the clinical range. The choice of cutpoints for the different scales was discussed in Chapters 2, 3, and 4.

For some practical and research purposes, users may wish to distinguish between pupils who are in the normal versus clinical range according to the cutpoints. Because categorical distinctions are usually least reliable for individuals who score close to the border of a category, we have identified a borderline clinical range for each scale. The addition of a borderline category often yields stronger associations between clinical status and classification of children according to their scale scores. This was demonstrated by phi correlations computed in our matched samples for the association between clinical status and scores trichotomized into the normal, borderline clinical, and clinical ranges, versus phi correlations for scores dichotomized into the normal and clinical range. In virtually all comparisons on all scales for each sex, the inclusion of the borderline range yielded higher phi correlations than did the dichotomous classification into the normal versus clinical range. Inclusion of the borderline category also yielded higher phi correlations for agreement between scores obtained from pairs of informants, including mother versus father, parent versus teacher, parent versus youth, and teacher versus youth (Achenbach, 1991a).

Despite the greater statistical power generally afforded by continuous quantitative scores and even by inclusion of a borderline range, users may wish to distinguish categorically between the normal and clinical range. The following sections report findings that indicate the degree to which classification of TRF scale scores as normal versus clinical distinguish between demographically matched nonreferred versus referred pupils.

Odds Ratios

One approach to analyzing associations between categorical classifications is by computing *relative risk odds ratios* (Fleiss, 1981), which are used in epidemiological research. The odds ratio indicates the odds that people who have a particular risk factor will also manifest a particular outcome, relative to the odds that people lacking the risk factor will manifest the outcome. The comparison between outcome rates for those who do and do not have the risk factor is expressed as the ratio of the odds of having the outcome if the risk factor is present, to the odds of having the outcome if the risk factor is absent. For example, a study of relations between smoking (a risk factor) and lung cancer (an outcome) may yield a relative risk odds ratio of 5.5. This means that people who smoke have 5.5 times greater odds of developing lung cancer than people who do not smoke.

We applied odds ratio analyses to the relations between TRF scores and referral status as follows: For each TRF scale, we first classified pupils from our matched nonreferred and referred samples according to whether they scored in the normal range or in the clinical range (including the borderline clinical range). Scoring in the clinical range on the TRF was thus equivalent to a "risk factor" in epidemiological research. We then computed the odds that pupils who scored in the clinical range on a particular scale were from the referred sample, relative to the odds for pupils who scored in the normal range. (Because referred pupils were already referred at the time the TRF was completed, we could also have made referral status the "risk factor" and TRF scores the "outcome variable." However, because we used odds ratios to indicate the strength of the contemporaneous association between TRF scores and referral status, rather than a predictive relation between a risk factor and a later outcome, the choice of the risk factor was not important and did not affect the obtained odds ratios.)

The relative risk odds ratio is a nonparametric statistic computed from a 2 x 2 table. We therefore included both sexes aged 5-18 in the same analysis to provide a summary odds ratio across all subjects. The statistical significance of the odds ratio is evaluated by computing confidence intervals.

Table 6-3 summarizes the odds ratios for relations between scale scores in the clinical range and referral status. Table 6-3 also shows the percent of referred and nonreferred pupils who scored in the clinical range according to cutpoints on the scales. Confidence intervals showed that all the odds ratios were significantly greater than 1.0, while chi squares showed that the differences between referred and nonreferred pupils scoring in the clinical range were significant in all comparisons ($p < .01$). The largest odds ratios were for having Academic Performance, the total adaptive score, and/or the total problem score in the clinical range (odds ratio = 13.0), Academic Performance scale alone (9.2), and the total adaptive score alone (8.6).

Combined Academic, Adaptive, and Problem Scores

Each adaptive item and syndrome score reflects deviance in a particular area that may characterize only a small proportion of referred pupils. The Academic Performance, total adaptive, and total problem scores, on the other hand, tap the full range of functioning assessed by the TRF. The less extreme clinical cutpoints for these scores automatically classify larger percents of both the referred and nonreferred samples as being in the clinical range than do the more extreme cutpoints of the syndrome scales. As Table 6-3 shows, 63% of referred pupils scored in the clinical range on the Academic Performance and

Table 6-3
Odds Ratios and Percent of Referred and
Nonreferred Samples Scoring in the TRF Clinical Range

Scale	Odds ratio	Percent in Clinical Range	
		Referred	Nonreferred
Academic Performance	9.2	63%	16%
Total Adaptive	8.6	63	17
Withdrawn	4.6	18	5
Somatic Complaints	2.4	11	5
Anxious/Depressed	6.1	24	5
Social Problems	8.3	30	5
Thought Problems	6.3	24	5
Attention Problems	8.4	30	5
Delinquent Behavior	7.0	26	5
Aggressive Behavior	7.8	29	5
Internalizing	4.8	50	17
Externalizing	5.8	56	18
Total Problems	8.3	64	17
≥1 Syndrome in Clinical Range	6.5	63	21
Int and/or Ext in Clinical Range	6.5	72	29
Academic, Adaptive and/or Probs in Clinical Range	13.0	84	29

Note. Total $N = 1,275$ referred and 1,275 demographically matched nonreferred pupils. In all analyses, the proportion of referred scoring in the clinical range was significantly greater than the proportion of nonreferred at $p < .01$ according to confidence intervals for odds ratios and Chi squares for 2 x 2 tables.

also on the total adaptive score, while 64% scored in the clinical range on the total problem score. This compares with 16% of the nonreferred pupils scoring in the clinical range on Academic Performance and 17% on both the total adaptive and total problem scores.

To simultaneously take account of deviance with respect to the cutpoints on the Academic Performance, total adaptive, and total problem scores, we classified pupils as deviant if they were deviant on any of these three scores and as nondeviant if they were in the normal range on all three scores. On this basis, 84% of the referred pupils and 29% of the nonreferred pupils were classified as deviant, as shown in Table 6-3. Combining the 16% of referred pupils classified as nondeviant ("false negatives") and the 29% of nonreferred pupils classified as deviant ("false positives") yielded an overall misclassification rate of (16% + 29%)/2 = 22.5%.

The combination of Academic Performance, total adaptive, and total problem scores can be used to create a borderline range that takes account of all three measures. This was done by classifying referred and nonreferred samples into the following three groups: *(a)* Nondeviant on all three scores; *(b)* deviant on one or two of the three scores; *(c)* deviant on all three scores. When this was done, 16% of the referred sample were included in category *a* (i.e., nondeviant on all three scores, or false negatives). Only 6% of the nonreferred sample were classified in category *c* (i.e., deviant on all three scores, or false positives). Another 35% of the subjects were classified in category *b* (i.e., deviant on one or two of the three scores).

Because it is seldom warranted to make a definitive clinical versus nonclinical judgment for every case on the basis of any single procedure, it is prudent to allow a borderline group. If the 35% who were deviant on one or two scores are regarded as a borderline group, the misclassification rate would be 16% false negatives + 6% false positives/2 = 11% total misclassification rate. The borderline group could be reduced substantially by combining pupils who were deviant on two scores with those who were deviant on all three. This reduced the borderline group to 18% and increased the false positives to 14%. Added to the 16% false negatives, the resulting overall misclassification rate was 15%, with 18% in the borderline group.

Discriminant Analyses

The foregoing sections dealt with the use of unweighted combinations of academic, adaptive, and problem scores to discriminate between pupils who were referred for help with behavioral/emotional problems versus pupils who were not referred. It is possible that weighted combinations of these three scores, all the scales, or items might produce better discrimination. To test this possibility, we performed discriminant analyses in which the criterion groups were the demographically matched referred and nonreferred pupils. Separate discriminant analyses were performed for each of the four sex/age groups.

The following three sets of discriminant analyses were performed for each group: *(a)* the Academic Performance, total adaptive, and total problem scores were used as predictors; *(b)* the Academic Performance, total adaptive, and all the syndrome scales were used as candidate predictors from which significant predictors were selected; *(c)* the Academic Performance score and all the individual adaptive and problem items were used as candidate predictors from which significant predictors were selected.

Discriminant analyses selectively weight predictors to maximize their collective associations with the particular criterion groups being analyzed. The weighting process makes use of characteristics of the sample that may differ from other samples. To avoid overestimating the accuracy of the classification obtained by discriminant analyses, it is therefore necessary to correct for the "shrinkage" in associations that would occur when discriminant weights derived in one sample are applied in a new sample. To correct for shrinkage, we employed a "jackknife" procedure whereby the discriminant function for each sample was computed multiple times with a different subject held out of the sample each time (SAS Institute, 1988). The discriminant function was then cross-validated multiple times by testing the accuracy of its prediction for each of the "hold-out" subjects. Finally, the percentage of correct predictions was averaged across all the hold-out subjects. It is these cross-validated predictions that we will present.

Academic, Adaptive, and Total Problem Scores.
Averaged across boys and girls, the mean misclassification rate
was 21.7%, with the percent of false negatives generally being
similar to the percent of false positives. The mean misclassification rate of 21.7% was only slightly better than the mean
misclassification rate of 22.5% obtained by classifying pupils
as normal if their (unweighted) Academic, total adaptive, and
total problem scores were all in the normal range and as
deviant if one or more scores were in the clinical range.
However, it was not as good as the 11% misclassification rate
obtained by allowing 35% borderline cases who were deviant
on up to two scores or the 15% misclassification rate obtained
with an 18% borderline group who were deviant on only one
score.

Scale Scores. When the Academic, total adaptive, and
syndrome scales were tested as candidate predictors, both the
academic and adaptive scales were retained as making significant ($p < .05$) independent contributions for all four sex/age
groups. Of the syndrome scales, only the Anxious/Depressed
and Delinquent Behavior syndromes were retained as significant predictors in at least two of the four groups, namely, the
12-18-year-olds of both sexes. The Aggressive Behavior
syndrome was the only significant syndrome predictor for 5-11-
year-old girls. For the other groups, the Withdrawn, Social
Problems, and Somatic Complaints syndromes were significant
predictors in one group each. The mean misclassification rate
averaged across the four sex/age groups was 20.7%, slightly
better than the 21.7% rate obtained in the discriminant analyses
using the total problem score with the Academic and total
adaptive scores.

Item Scores. When Academic Performance, the individual
adaptive items, and problem items were tested as candidate
predictors, Academic Performance was again retained as a
significant predictor in all four sex/age groups. It accounted

for more variance than any other item in the discriminant
function for three groups and the second most variance for 12-
18-year-old boys, for whom it was second to Item *25. Doesn't
get along with other pupils.* Teachers' ratings of how happy
the pupil was also contributed significantly to discrimination
between referred and nonreferred pupils in all four groups. The
problem items retained as significant predictors varied considerably among the four groups. The number of significant
problem items ranged from 8 to 13. The ones that were
significant for as many as two groups were: *17. Daydreams or
gets lost in his/her thoughts; 22. Difficulty following directions;
81. Feels hurt when criticized;* and *84. Strange behavior.* The
mean misclassification rate was 18%, which is still not as good
as the 15% obtained when a borderline group of 18% was
allowed.

PROBABILITY OF PARTICULAR SCORES
BEING FROM THE REFERRED VERSUS
NONREFERRED SAMPLES

To provide a further picture of relations between particular
scores and referral status, Table 6-4 displays the probability of
particular Academic Performance and total adaptive T scores
being from our referred samples, while Table 6-5 displays
similar relations for the total problem scores. The probabilities
were determined by tabulating the proportion of pupils from
our matched referred and nonreferred samples who had scores
within each of the intervals shown. T scores were used to
provide a uniform metric for the four sex/age groups. Because
the T scores for the Academic Performance and total adaptive
scores were truncated at the top and bottom, raw scores might
provide better discrimination between referred and nonreferred
samples at the extremes of these distributions than T scores do.
Nevertheless, as can be seen from Table 6-4, the probability of
the lowest possible T score being from the referred sample was

quite high for all groups. Conversely, the probability of the highest possible T score being from the referred group was quite low. Because the T scores for the total problem scores were not truncated, they are highly correlated with the raw total problem scores.

Table 6-4
Probability of TRF Academic Performance or
Total Adaptive Scores Being from Referred Sample

| | Boys | | | | Girls | | | |
| | 5-11 | | 12-18 | | 5-11 | | 12-18 | |
T Score	Acad	Adapt	Acad	Adapt	Acad	Adapt	Acad	Adapt
N =	664	659	476	481	727	725	569	574
35	.88	.85	.78	.85	.88	.86	.91	.91
36	.82	.86	.64	.80	.70	.84	.70	.75
37-40[a]	.50	.62	.61	.65	.52	.61	.69	.68
41-44	.40	.59	.64	.52	.29	.42	.44	.51
45-48	.38	.37	.40	.46	.33	.36	.38	.32
49-52	.21	.28	.32	.23	.24	.35	.33	.26
53-56	.22	.19	.20	.30	.31	.12	.18	.20
57-60	.18	.22	.21	.19	.19	.15	.16	.07
61-64	.21	.12	.09	.07	.14	.13	.09	.05
65	.12	.13	.10	.15	.04	.11	.03	.00

Note. Samples were demographically matched referred and nonreferred pupils. Ns were reduced from total sample by a lack of scores for some subjects.
[a]T scores ≤ 40 are in the clinical range.

As both tables show, once a probability of .50 was reached, the probabilities of all scores on one side of this point were all >.50., whereas the probabilities of all scores on the other side of this point were <.50. Users can refer to the tables to estimate the likelihood that particular Academic Performance, total adaptive, and total problem scores represent deviance severe enough to warrant concern.

Table 6-5
Probability of TRF Total Problems Score
Being from Referred Sample

T Score	Boys 5-11	Boys 12-18	Girls 5-11	Girls 12-18
N =	668	518	758	606
0 - 35	.09	.10	.18	.09
36 - 39	.22	.07	.08	.00
40 - 43	.12	.03	.18	.05
44 - 47	.21	.16	.21	.19
48 - 51	.24	.28	.37	.21
52 - 55	.43	.42	.41	.35
56 - 59	.54	.55	.52	.48
60[a]- 63	.70	.73	.48	.67
64 - 67	.72	.70	.84	.77
68 - 71	.77	.88	.80	.95
72 - 75	.90	.89	.87	.86
76 -100	.97	.86	.94	.90

Note. Samples were demographically matched referred and nonreferred pupils.
[a]T scores ≥ 60 are in the clinical range.

SUMMARY

This chapter presented several kinds of evidence for the validity of TRF scores. *Content validity* is supported by the ability of most TRF items to discriminate significantly between demographically matched referred and nonreferred pupils (documented by analyses presented in Chapter 7). *Criterion-related* validity is supported by the ability of the TRF's quantitative scale scores to discriminate between referred and nonreferred pupils with demographic effects partialled out. Clinical cutpoints on the scale scores were also shown to discriminate significantly between demographically matched referred and nonreferred pupils.

Several procedures were presented for discriminating between pupils like those in our referred versus nonreferred samples. One of the most effective ways to optimize discrimination is by classifying pupils as nondeviant if their Academic, total adaptive, and total problem scores are all in the normal range and as deviant if all three scores are in the clinical range. Pupils who are in the normal range on one or two scores are then classified as borderline between the two groups that are more clearly deviant or nondeviant. By classifying pupils as deviant if any two of the three scales are in the clinical range, the borderline group could be reduced to 18% while still obtaining a good overall misclassification rate of 15%.

Findings from discriminant analyses indicated the individual scales and items that contributed the most discriminative power when compared with all other scales or items.

Chapter 7
Item Scores

Beside being the basis for the TRF profile scales, the TRF items provide scores for specific adaptive characteristics and problems, as reported by teachers. To determine which items discriminated significantly between children referred for mental health or special education services and nonreferred children, we performed analyses of covariance (ANCOVA) on the item scores obtained by the demographically matched samples described in Chapter 6. The ANCOVA design was 2 (referral status) x 2 (sex) x 6 (ages 5-7, 8-9, 10-11, 12-13, 14-15, 16-18). The number of subjects per cell ranged from 74 for 16-18-year-old boys to 141 for 5-7-year-old girls, with a mean of 106 children per cell. The total N was 2,550, with equal numbers of demographically-matched referred and nonreferred children. SES was covaried using the 9-step Hollingshead (1975) scores for parental occupation. Ethnicity was covaried by creating a dummy variable scored 1 for white versus 0 for nonwhite and a second dummy variable scored 1 for black versus 0 for nonblack. There were not enough children of any other ethnic group to warrant creating an additional dummy variable for another ethnic group.

ACADEMIC AND ADAPTIVE SCORES

As reported in Chapter 6, academic performance and the sum of the four adaptive characteristics were included in the regression analyses of scale scores, but they were also included in the ANCOVAs reported here to provide direct comparisons with the four adaptive characteristics in the same analytic design. The scores were computed as they are on the TRF profile, i.e., the mean of scores 1-5 for the teacher's ratings of performance in each academic subject, scores 1-7 for the four adaptive characteristics, and the sum of the four adaptive characteristics. Appendix A provides the scoring rules.

Table 7-1 displays the ANCOVA results in terms of the percent of variance accounted for by each effect that was significant at $p < .01$. According to Cohen's (1988) criteria for the magnitude of effects in ANCOVA, effects accounting for 1 to 5.9% of variance are considered small, effects accounting for 5.9 to 13.8% of variance are medium, and effects accounting for $>13.8\%$ are large. Although there were only six ANCOVAs, we have taken the precaution of indicating with superscript g the one out of six effects of each independent variable and covariate that was most likely to be significant by chance, because it had the smallest F value (Sakoda et al., 1954). Out of the 24 possible 2- and 3-way interactions, only one was significant, and it accounted for $<1\%$ of variance. Because this is less than would be expected by chance in 24 statistical tests, the interactions are omitted from Table 7-1.

As Table 7-1 shows, referral status had a large effect on all six academic and adaptive scores, with referred children obtaining lower scores than nonreferred children. The effects ranged from 15% of variance in ratings of how hard the child was working, to 25% for the sum of the four adaptive characteristics. Because the effect on "working hard" was the smallest, it is marked by superscript g to indicate that it is the one most likely to be significant by chance. However, its F value was 464.3, $p = .0001$. Applying the Bonferroni procedure of multiplying the p value by 6 to reflect the number of comparisons still yields $p = .0006$, indicating that it was very unlikely to be a chance effect. All six scores thus discriminated very well between referred and nonreferred children. The relations between age, sex, and referral status can be seen for the four adaptive characteristics in Figure 7-1, where the data points correspond to the cells of the 2 x 2 x 6 ANCOVAs.

Table 7-1
Percent of Variance Accounted for by Significant ($p < .01$) Effects of
Referral Status and Demographic Variables in ANCOVAs on Academic
and Adaptive Scores

Item	Ref Stat[a]	Sex[b]	Age[c]	Covariates SES[d]	White[e]	Black[f]
VII. Academic Performance	24	1	$<1^{NLg}$	5	--	--
VIII. 1. Working Hard	15[g]	2	--	2	--	<1
2. Behaving Appropriately	20	4	$<1^{O}$	<1[g]	--	<1
3. Learning	21	1	--	3	--	<1[g]
4. Happy	22	<1[g]	--	1	<1[g]	<1
Total Adaptive	25	2	--	2	--	<1

Note. $N = 2{,}550$ demographically matched referred and nonreferred 5- to 18-year-olds. Interactions are not shown because only 1 out of 24 was significant, which is less than expected by chance.
[a]All scores were higher for nonreferred than referred.
[b]All scores were higher for girls than boys.
[c]NL = nonlinear effect of age; O = older scored higher.
[d]All scores were higher for upper SES.
[e]The one significant effect indicated higher scores for white than nonwhite.
[f]All significant effects indicated higher scores for nonblack than black.
[g]Not significant when corrected for number of analyses.

(Similar figures for Academic Performance and the sum of the adaptive characteristics were presented in Chapter 6.)

Demographic Differences in Academic and Adaptive Scores

Table 7-1 shows that girls were rated significantly higher than boys on all six academic and adaptive scores. The effect sizes were all small, ranging from <1% of variance for ratings of how happy the child was, to 4% for how appropriately the child was behaving. However, they do indicate that teachers generally view girls as functioning somewhat better than boys.

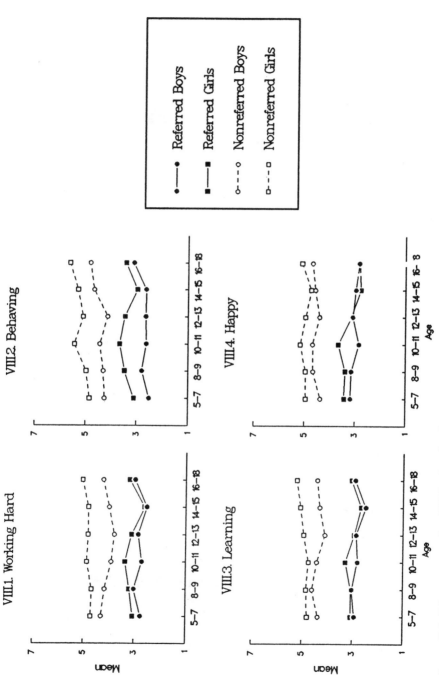

Figure 7-1. Mean scores for TRF adaptive items.

The two significant age effects accounted for <1% of variance. One was a nonlinear effect reflecting a tendency for ages 12-13 and 14-15 to obtain lower scores for academic performance than younger or older children. The fact that the academic performance scores increased significantly at ages 16-18 suggests that pupils whose academic performance is poor at ages 12-15 are likely to leave school at age 16, thereby causing the mean academic score to be higher at ages 16-18, because the better students tend to remain beyond 16. The other very small age effect reflected a tendency for ratings of "behaving appropriately" to be slightly higher for older than younger children.

All SES effects indicated small tendencies for teachers to rate upper SES pupils more favorably than lower SES pupils. The largest effect accounted for 5% of the variance in academic performance, while the smallest accounted for <1% of the variance in "appropriately behaving."

No effects of ethnicity accounted for as much as 1% of the variance. The covariate comparing whites and nonwhites showed that whites were rated slightly higher on "how happy" the child was. The covariate comparing blacks and nonblacks showed that blacks were rated slightly lower on the four adaptive characteristics and the sum of these four, but that there was no significant difference in academic performance.

PROBLEM ITEM SCORES

The 0-1-2 scores on the problem items were analyzed for the 2,550 matched referred and nonreferred children, using the same 2 (referral status) x 2 (sex) x 6 (age) ANCOVA design as was used for adaptive functioning. SES, white versus non-white, and black versus nonblack were the covariates, as they were in the ANCOVAs of adaptive functioning. Table 7-2 displays the ANCOVA results in terms of the percent of variance that was accounted for by each effect that was significant at $p <.01$. To take account of findings that might be significant by chance, we have indicated with superscript g the 5 out of 120 tests of each independent variable and covariate that were most likely to be significant by chance, because they had the smallest F values (Sakoda et al., 1954).

Referral Status Differences in Problem Scores

Table 7-2 shows that referred children obtained significantly ($p <.01$) higher scores on all problem items except Items *32, 47, 56e, 56g, 75,* and *113*. Even on the latter items, referred children also obtained higher scores than nonreferred children, with the differences on Items *47, 56g,* and *113* being significant at $p <.05$.

Differences between referred and nonreferred children had a large effect on the total problem score, accounting for 23% of variance. These differences were not affected by any interactions with demographic variables, although teachers reported slightly more problems for boys than girls (2% of variance), lower SES than upper SES (1% of variance), and blacks than nonblacks (<1% of variance).

The following items showed large effects (>13.8% of variance) of referral status, with the effect size indicated in parentheses: *22. Difficulty following directions* (15% of variance); *25. Doesn't get along with other pupils* (14%); and *49. Has difficulty learning* (16%). As Table 7-2 shows, all demographic effects associated with these items were very small. Of the significant ($p <.01$) effects of referral status on the other items, 48 were medium, 51 were small, and 12 accounted for <1% of variance.

To provide a detailed picture of the prevalence rate for each problem item, Figure 7-2 displays the percent of children for whom each problem was reported (i.e., was scored 1 or 2). The data points correspond to the cells of the ANCOVAs, with children grouped according to referral status, sex, and age. (A

Table 7-2

Percent of Variance Accounted for by Significant (p <.01) Effects of Referral Status and Demographic Variables on TRF Problem Scores

Item	Ref Stat[a]	Sex[b]	Age[c]	Interactions[d] RxS	RxA	SxA	Covariates SES[e]	Black[f]
1. Acts too young	9	2M	<1Y	--	--	--	<1	--
2. Hums	5	4M	3Y	--	<1	--	<1	<1
3. Argues	9	<1M	--	<1g	--	--	--	<1
4. Fails to finish	9	2M	--	--	--	--	<1	<1
5. Behaves like opposite sex	<1g	--	--	--	--	--	<1g	--
6. Defiant	11	1M	1O	--	--	--	<1	--
7. Brags	4	2M	<1NLg	--	<1	--	--	<1
8. Can't concentrate	13	2M	<1Y	--	--	<1	<1	<1
9. Can't get mind off thoughts	6	--	--	--	--	--	--	--
10. Can't sit still	8	3M	2Y	--	<1	--	<1	--
11. Too dependent	7	<1F	<1Y	--	--	--	<1	--
12. Lonely	3	--	--	--	--	--	<1	--
13. Confused	9	<1M	--	--	--	--	<1	--
14. Cries a lot	4	<1F	1Y	<1g	--	--	--	<1
15. Fidgets	8	2M	2Y	--	<1	--	--	<1
16. Mean to others	8	1M	<1NL	<1	--	--	<1	<1
17. Daydreams	5	1M	--	--	--	--	<1	--
18. Harms self	2	--	--	--	<1g	<1	<1	--
19. Demands attention	13	<1M	<1Y	--	--	--	<1	<1g
20. Destroys own things	5	2M	1Y	<1	<1	--	<1	--

Table 7-2 (Continued)

Item	Ref Stat[a]	Sex[b]	Age[c]	Interactions[d]			Covariates	
				RxS	RxA	SxA	SES[e]	Black[f]
21. Destroys others' things	5	2^M	--	<1	--	--	--	--
22. Difficulty with directions	15	1^M	1^Y	--	--	--	<1	$<1^g$
23. Disobeys	11	3^M	--	<1	--	<1	<1	<1
24. Disturbs others	11	4^M	$<1^Y$	--	--	--	<1	$<1^g$
25. Doesn't get along	14	$<1^M$	$<1^{NL}$	--	$<1^g$	--	$<1^g$	--
26. Lacks guilt	9	2^M	$<1^{NL}$	--	--	--	<1	<1
27. Jealous	5	--	--	--	--	$<1^g$	--	--
28. Eats nonfood	1	--	--	--	--	--	--	--
29. Fears	2	--	--	--	--	--	--	--
30. Fears school	2	--	--	--	--	<1	--	--
31. Fears impulses	2	--	--	--	--	--	--	--
32. Needs to be perfect	--	--	--	--	--	--	$<1^U$	--
33. Feels unloved	6	$<1^{Fg}$	1^O	--	--	--	<1	--
34. Feels persecuted	8	$<1^M$	2^O	--	--	--	<1	--
35. Feels worthless	9	--	$<1^{NLg}$	--	--	--	<1	--
36. Accident-prone	2	--	$<1^{NL}$	--	--	--	<1	--
37. Fighting	10	1^M	2^O	<1	--	<1	<1	--
38. Is teased	7	--	--	--	--	--	--	--
39. Hangs around kids who get in trouble	6	3^M	2^O	--	<1	--	<1	--
40. Hears things	2	--	--	--	--	--	--	--
41. Acts without thinking	12	2^M	--	--	--	--	<1	--

Table 7-2 (Continued)

Item	Ref Stat[a]	Sex[b]	Age[c]	Interactions[d]			Covariates	
				RxS	RxA	SxA	SES[e]	Black[f]
42. Would rather be alone	4	<1M	<1O	--	<1	--	--	--
43. Lying, cheating	9	<1M	--	--	--	--	<1	--
44. Bites fingernails	3	--	<1NL	--	<1g	<1g	<1	--
45. Nervous	10	<1M	--	--	--	<1	<1	--
46. Nervous movements	4	1M	--	<1	--	--	--	--
47. Overconforms	--	--	--	--	--	--	--	--
48. Not liked	9	--	<1NLg	--	--	--	--	<1
49. Difficulty learning	16	<1M	--	--	--	--	2	--
50. Fearful, anxious	7	--	--	--	--	--	--	--
51. Dizzy	<1	--	<1NL	--	--	--	--	--
52. Feels too guilty	2	2M	1Y	--	--	--	<1	<1
53. Talks out of turn	8	1M	<1NL	--	--	--	1	<1
54. Overtired	3	<1M	1O	--	--	--	--	--
55. Overweight	<1	<1F	--	<1g	--	--	<1	--
56a. Aches, pains	1	<1F	<1NLg	--	--	--	<1	--
56b. Headaches	<1g	<1F	--	--	--	--	--	--
56c. Nausea, feels sick	<1	--	--	--	--	--	--	--
56d. Eye problems	<1g	--	--	--	--	--	--	--
56e. Skin problems	--	--	--	<1	--	--	--	--
56f. Stomachaches	<1g	<1F	--	<1	--	--	--	--
56g. Vomiting	--	--	--	<1	--	<1	--	--
56h. Other physical problems	<1	--	--	--	--	--	--	--

Table 7-2 (Continued)

Item	Ref Stat[a]	Sex[b]	Age[c]	Interactions[d]			Covariates	
				RxS	RxA	SxA	SES[e]	Black[f]
57. Attacks people	7	1[M]	--	<1	--	--	<1	--
58. Picking	3	<1[M]	<1[Y]	--	--	--	<1	--
59. Sleeps in class	<1	1[M]	3[O]	--	--	1	<1	<1
60. Apathetic	6	1[M]	1[O]	--	--	--	1	<1
61. Poor school work	11	2[M]	--	--	--	--	2	<1
62. Clumsy	6	<1[M]	1[Y]	--	<1[g]	--	--	--
63. Prefers older kids	3	<1[M]	2[O]	<1	1	--	--	--
64. Prefers younger kids	3	--	1[Y]	--	--	--	--	--
65. Refuses to talk	4	--	--	--	--	--	<1[g]	--
66. Repeats acts	3	<1[M]	--	--	--	--	--	--
67. Disrupts class	9	3[M]	<1[NL]	--	--	--	<1	<1
68. Screams a lot	5	--	--	--	--	--	--	--
69. Secretive	4	--	<1[O]	--	--	--	<1	--
70. Sees things	<1[g]	--	--	--	--	--	--	--
71. Self-conscious	1	<1[Fg]	--	--	--	--	--	--
72. Messy work	6	3[M]	2[Y]	--	--	--	<1	--
73. Irresponsible	8	2[M]	--	<1[g]	--	--	<1[g]	--
74. Shows off	4	8[M]	--	--	--	--	--	<1[g]
75. Shy	--	<1[F]	--	--	--	--	--	--
76. Explosive	11	<1[M]	<1[Og]	<1	--	--	<1	--
77. Easily frustrated	13	<1[M]	--	--	--	--	<1	--
78. Inattentive	13	2[M]	--	--	--	--	1	<1

Table 7-2 (Continued)

Item	Ref Stat[a]	Sex[b]	Age[c]	Interactions[d]			Covariates	
				RxS	RxA	SxA	SES[e]	Black[f]
79. Speech problem	5	$<1^{M}$	2^{Y}	--	--	--	--	--
80. Stares blankly	5	$<1^{M}$	--	--	--	--	1	--
81. Feels hurt when criticized	6	--	$<1^{NL}$	--	--	--	--	--
82. Steals	4	$<1^{Mg}$	--	--	--	--	--	--
83. Stores up unneeded things	1	--	1^{Y}	--	--	--	--	--
84. Strange behavior	7	$<1^{M}$	--	$<1^{g}$	--	--	<1	<1
85. Strange ideas	4	1^{M}	--	<1	--	--	<1	$<1^{g}$
86. Stubborn	12	$<1^{M}$	--	--	--	--	<1	<1
87. Moody	12	--	$<1^{NL}$	--	--	--	<1	--
88. Sulks a lot	10	$<1^{Mg}$	1^{O}	--	<1	--	<1	--
89. Suspicious	7	1^{M}	2^{O}	--	1	--	1	--
90. Swearing	8	1^{M}	--	<1	1^{g}	--	1	--
91. Suicidal talk	2	2^{M}	--	--	$<1^{g}$	--	--	--
92. Underachieving	9	2^{M}	1^{O}	--	--	--	<1	<1
93. Talks too much	4	$<1^{M}$	$<1^{Y}$	--	--	--	<1	<1
94. Teases a lot	5	2^{M}	1^{NL}	<1	--	$<1^{g}$	<1	--
95. Temper tantrums	10	$<1^{M}$	$<1^{O}$	--	1	$<1^{g}$	--	<1
96. Thinks about sex	4	1^{M}	2^{O}	--	1	--	<1	--
97. Threatens people	8	--	1^{O}	<1	1	--	--	<1
98. Tardy	2	--	3°	--	--	--	--	--
99. Concerned with neat, clean	<1	2^{M}	--	--	--	--	<1	<1
100. Fails to carry out tasks	9	--	--	--	--	--	<1	<1

Table 7-2 (Continued)

Item	Ref Stat[a]	Sex[b]	Age[c]	Interactions[d] RxS	RxA	SxA	Covariates SES[e]	Black[f]
101. Truancy	2	--	3°	--	<1	--	2	--
102. Lacks energy	5	<1^M	--	--	--	--	<1	--
103. Unhappy, sad, depressed	13	--	<1^O	--	--	<1^g	<1	<1
104. Loud	7	<1^Mg	--	--	--	--	--	--
105. Alcohol, drugs	3	<1^M	8°	--	4	--	<1	--
106. Anxious to please	<1	--	--	--	--	<1	--	--
107. Dislikes school	4	<1^M	5°	--	<1	--	1	--
108. Fears mistakes	2	--	--	--	<1	--	--	--
109. Whining	4	--	--	--	--	--	--	<1
110. Unclean	4	--	--	--	--	--	2	--
111. Withdrawn	5	--	<1^O	--	--	--	<1^g	--
112. Worries	4	--	--	--	--	--	--	--
113. Other problems	--	<1^M	--	--	--	--	--	--
Total Problems	23	2^M	--	--	--	--	1	<1

Note. $N = 2,550$ demographically matched referred and nonreferred 5- to 18-year-olds. Effects of 3-way interactions and the white vs. nonwhite covariate are omitted because they were minimal, as discussed in text.

[a] All scores were higher for referred than nonreferred. Differences on Items 47, 56g, and 113 were significant at $p < .05$ but not $p < .01$. [b] F = females scored higher; M = males scored higher. [c] NL = nonlinear effect of age; O = older scored higher; Y = younger scored higher. [d] RxS = referral status x sex; RxA = referral status x age; SxA = sex x age. [e] Except Item 32 (superscripted U), all significant effects indicated higher scores for lower SES. [f] All significant effects indicated higher scores for black than nonblack. [g] Not significant when corrected for number of analyses.

figure displaying the mean total problem scores was presented in Chapter 6.)

Demographic Differences in Problem Scores

Table 7-2 displays significant effects of sex and age, 2-way interactions, and the covariates of SES and black versus nonblack ethnicity. The 3-way interactions are not displayed, because only four were significant, which is fewer than the five expected by chance. All four 3-way interactions accounted for <1% of variance. The white-nonwhite covariate is not displayed, either, because there were only 14 significant effects out of 120 and all accounted for <1% of variance. Excluding the five significant effects expected by chance, whites received higher scores on Items *17, 35, 45, 62, 80, 103*, and *112*, whereas nonwhites received higher scores on Items *8* and *63*. All 30 effects of the black-nonblack covariate reflected higher scores for blacks, but all accounted for <1% of the variance, as shown in Table 7-2.

Boys obtained higher scores on 65 items and the total problem score. The only sex difference exceeding Cohen's criterion for small effects was on Item *74. Showing off or clowning*, where the tendency for boys to score higher accounted for 8% of variance. This item also showed the largest sex difference in parents' CBCL ratings and the largest effect among items on which boys rated themselves higher than girls on the YSR (Achenbach, 1991b, 1991c). Girls obtained higher scores on nine items, with the sex difference accounting for <1% of variance in each of them. Of the 14 Internalizing items showing significant sex differences, girls and boys were each scored higher on 7. All 29 of the Externalizing items, by contrast, were scored higher for boys than girls. The tendency for boys to score higher on Externalizing items was significant, $\chi^2 = 17.32$, $p < .001$.

Linear age effects indicated significantly higher scores for older children on 24 items and for younger children on 19. An

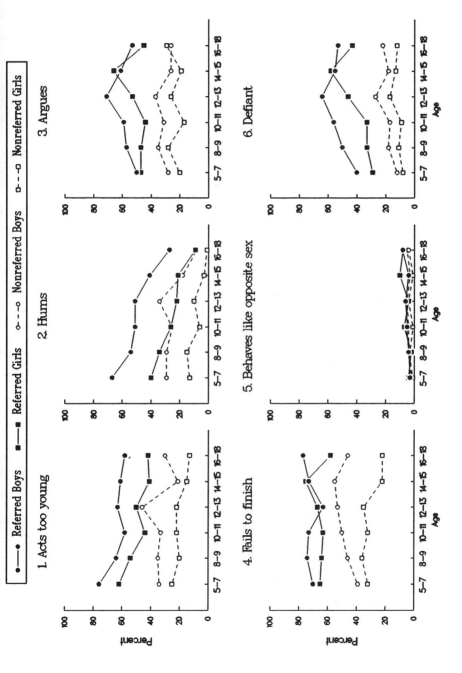

Figure 7-2. Percent of pupils for whom each TRF problem item was reported.

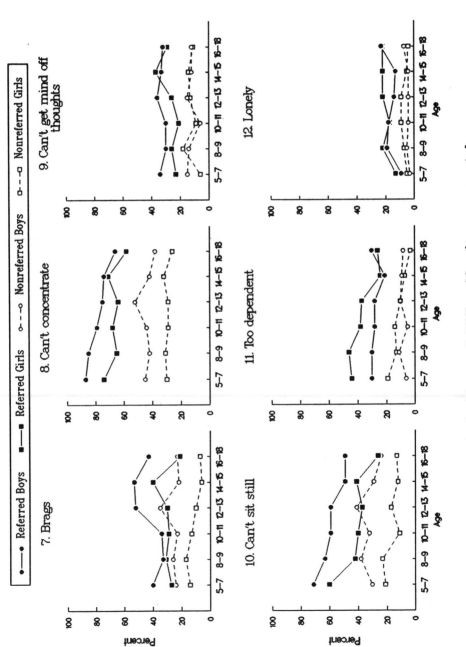

Figure 7-2 (cont). Percent of pupils for whom each TRF problem item was reported.

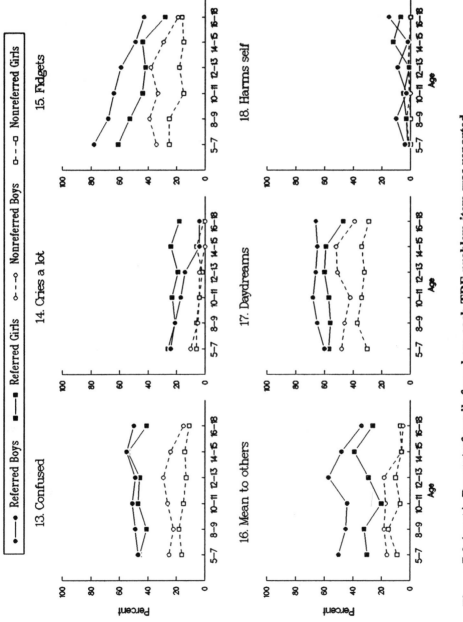

Figure 7-2 (cont.). Percent of pupils for whom each TRF problem item was reported.

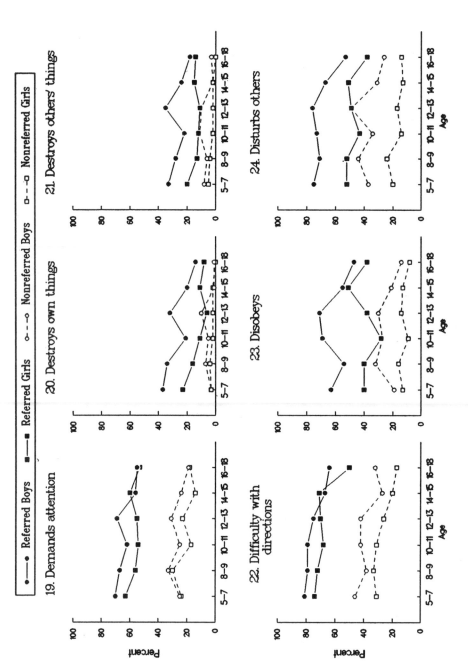

Figure 7-2 (cont.). Percent of pupils for whom each TRF problem item was reported.

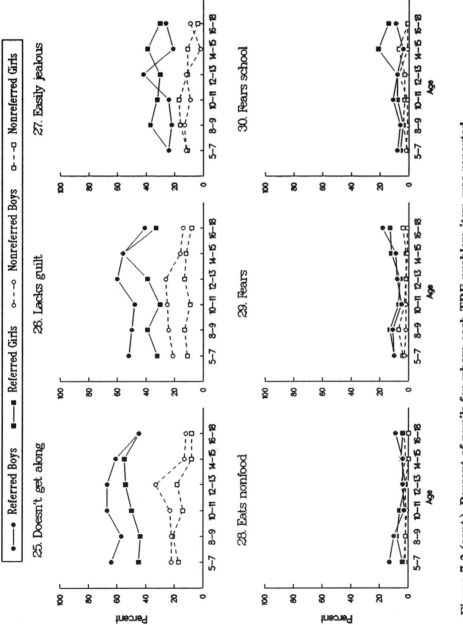

Figure 7-2 (cont.). Percent of pupils for whom each TRF problem item was reported.

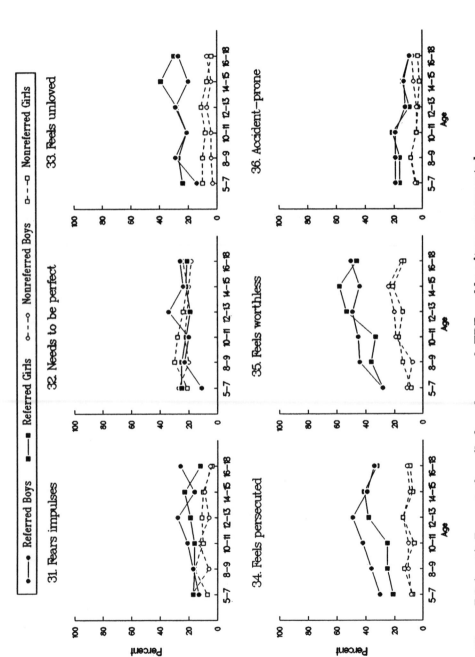

Figure 7-2 (cont.). Percent of pupils for whom each TRF problem item was reported.

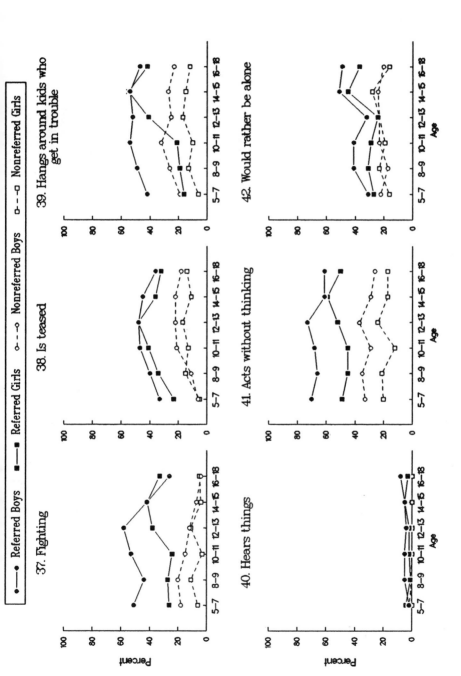

Figure 7-2 (cont.). Percent of pupils for whom each TRF problem item was reported.

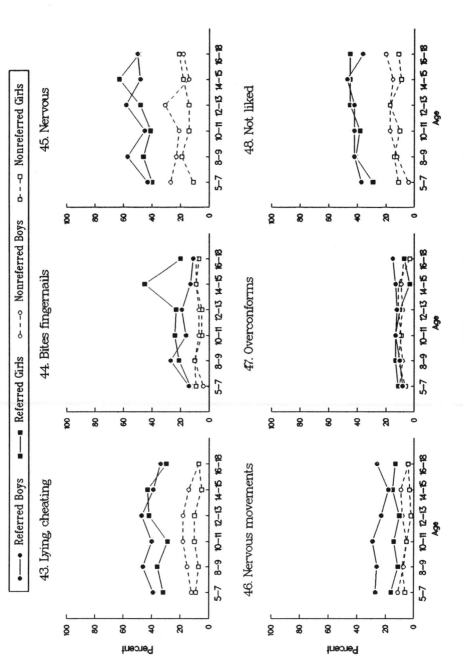

Figure 7-2 (cont.). Percent of pupils for whom each TRF problem item was reported.

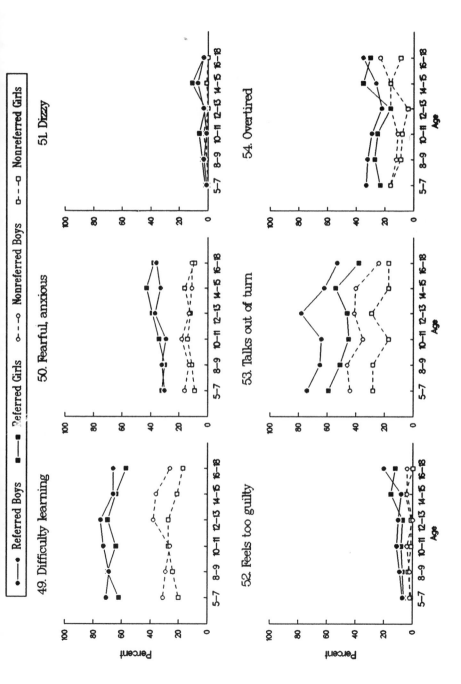

Figure 7-2 (cont.). Percent of pupils for whom each TRF problem item was reported.

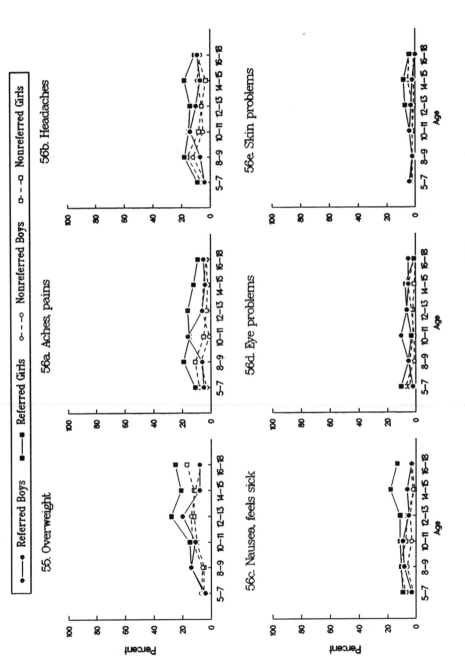

Figure 7-2 (cont.). Percent of pupils for whom each TRF problem item was reported.

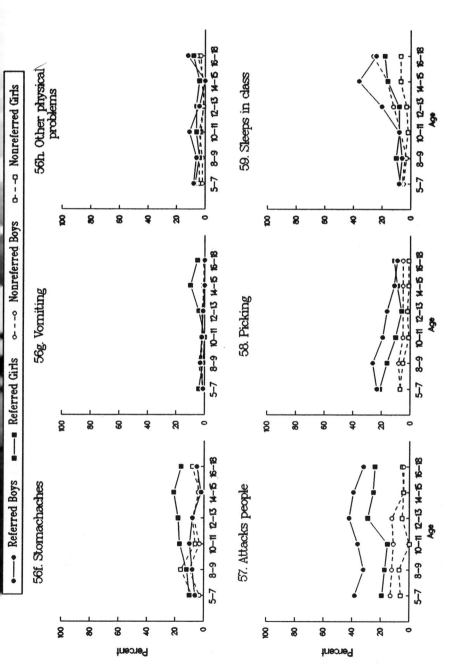

Figure 7-2 (cont.). Percent of pupils for whom each TRF problem item was reported.

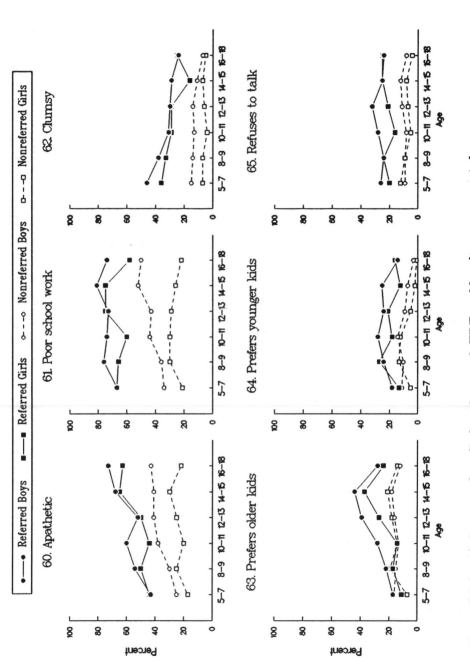

Figure 7-2 (cont.). Percent of pupils for whom each TRF problem item was reported.

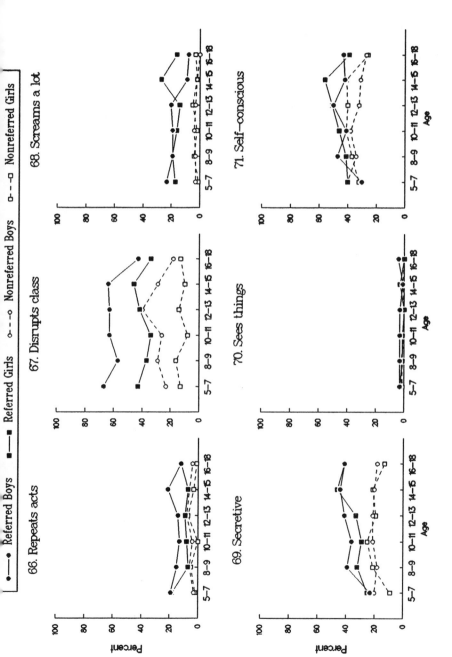

Figure 7-2 (cont.). Percent of pupils for whom each TRF problem item was reported.

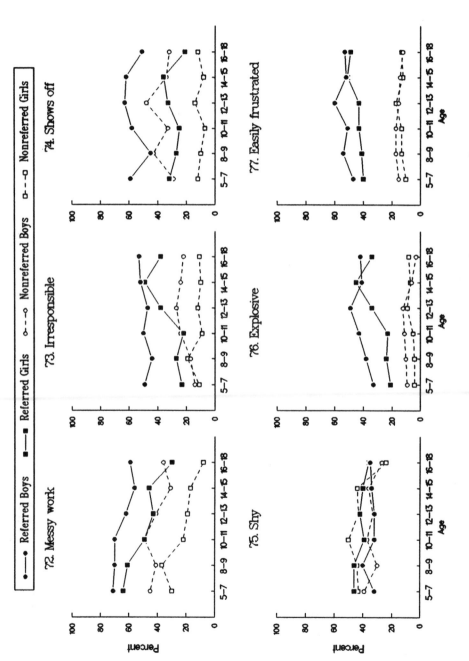

Figure 7-2 (cont.). Percent of pupils for whom each TRF problem item was reported.

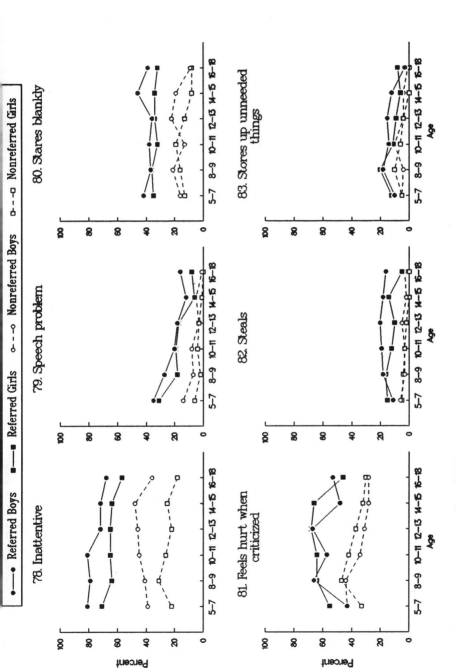

Figure 7-2 (cont). Percent of pupils for whom each TRF problem item was reported.

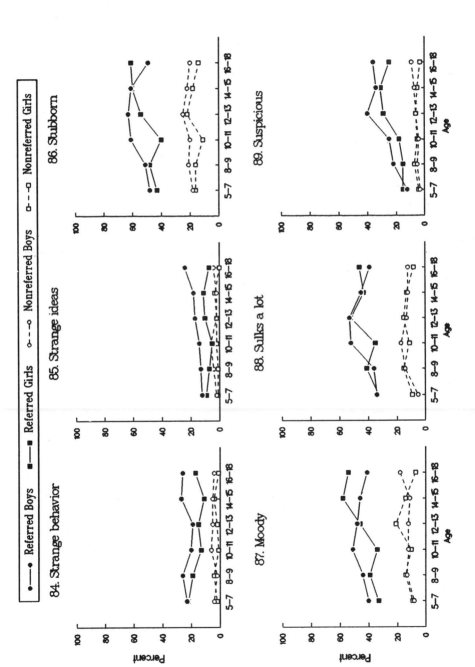

Figure 7-2 (cont.). Percent of pupils for whom each TRF problem item was reported.

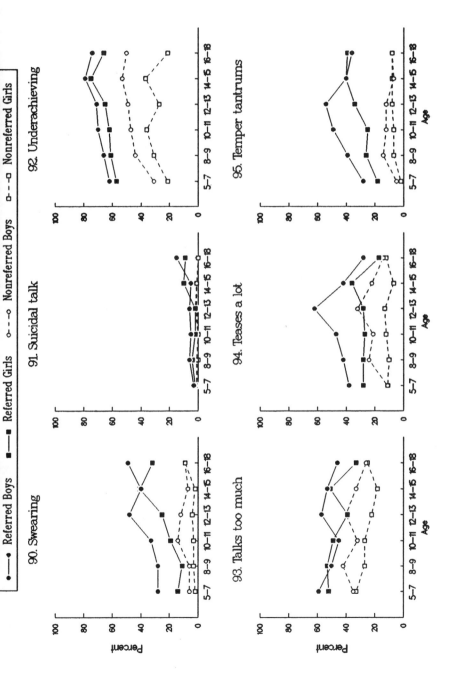

Figure 7-2 (cont.). Percent of pupils for whom each TRF problem item was reported.

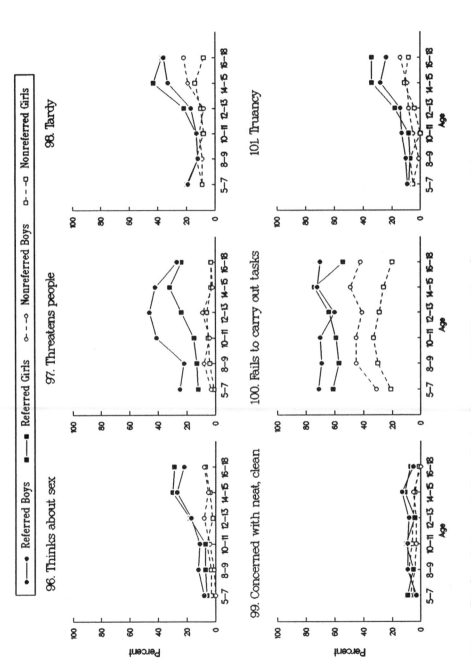

Figure 7-2 (cont.). Percent of pupils for whom each TRF problem item was reported.

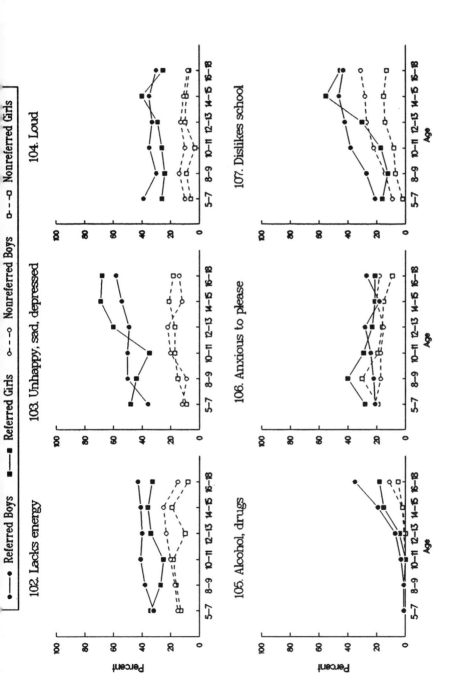

Figure 7-2 (cont.). Percent of pupils for whom each TRF problem item was reported.

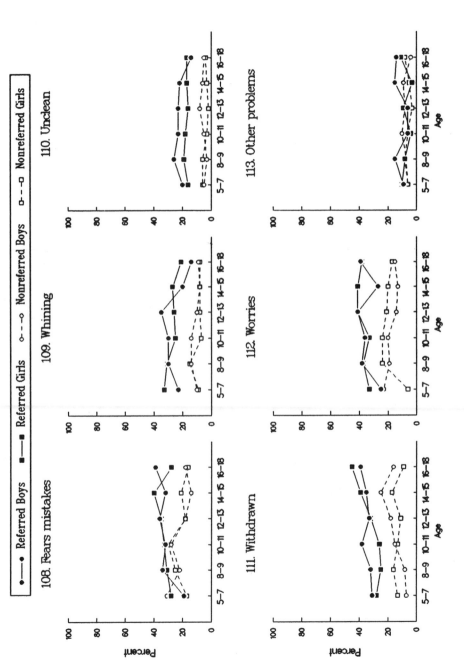

Figure 7-2 (cont). Percent of pupils for whom each TRF problem item was reported.

additional 15 items showed nonlinear effects of age, as indicated by the superscript *NL* in Table 7-2. The shapes of these age effects can be seen from the graphs of the item scores in Figure 7-2. The largest age effect accounted for 8% of the variance in Item *105. Uses alcohol or drugs for nonmedical purposes*, where older children scored higher. No other age differences exceeded Cohen's criteria for small effects. There was no significant difference between the proportion of Internalizing versus Externalizing items that were scored higher for younger versus older children.

The only 2-way interaction that accounted for >1% of variance was on Item *105*. This interaction reflected much higher scores for referred than nonreferred children at ages 14-15 and 16-18, in contrast to smaller differences in the younger age groups.

Significant SES effects reflected higher scores for lower SES children on 65 items and total problems, in contrast to higher scores for upper SES children only on Item *32. Feels he/she has to be perfect*. The tendency for lower SES children to obtain higher scores accounted for >1% of the variance in Items *49, 61, 101,* and *110*. The proportion of Externalizing items scored higher for lower SES children was significantly higher than the proportion of Internalizing items, $\chi^2 = 7.25$, $p < .01$.

SUMMARY

This chapter reported ANCOVAs of scores obtained by matched referred and nonreferred children on the TRF academic and adaptive items and scales, problem items, and total problem score. All the academic and adaptive scores showed large effects of referral status (referred children scored lower), plus small effects of sex (boys scored lower) and SES (lower SES scored lower).

All problem items and the total problem score were higher for referred than nonreferred children, with most of the differences being significant. Boys and lower SES children tended to obtain higher problem scores than girls and upper SES children, especially on Externalizing items.

Chapter 8
Relations Between Pre-1991
and 1991 TRF Scales

This chapter summarizes differences between the pre-1991 and 1991 TRF scales, the scales having counterparts in the two editions, and correlations between the counterpart scales.

Beside the differences in the scales themselves, an innovation applied to all the 1991 scales is the designation of a borderline range adjoining the clinical cutpoint. The purpose is to emphasize that all scores are subject to variation and that a clinical cutpoint does not mark a definitive boundary between the normal and abnormal. For purposes of statistical analysis, a specific cutpoint is specified for each scale, but clinical evaluations of individual children whose scores are among the four T scores of the borderline range should emphasize that they are in the borderline clinical range.

Additional innovations include the following:

1. Normalized T scores were based on the midpoints between percentiles of the raw score distributions.

2. All syndrome scales were truncated at $T = 50$, rather than 55 to 59 as on the pre-1991 scales.

3. Gaps of more than 5 points between $T = 50$ and the next higher T score were limited by using the mean of $T = 50$ and the third highest T score.

4. $T = 89$ was assigned to the mean of the five highest raw scores obtained by our clinical samples on the Internal-

izing, Externalizing, and total problem scores, rather than to the highest scores, as were used to establish T = 89 on the pre-1991 scales.

5. On the hand-scored profiles, scale scores for the two age groups of boys are listed side-by-side, as are scores for the two age groups of girls. Users should be careful to select the column of scores designated for the age of the child being scored.

6. Internalizing and Externalizing scores can be computed from scale scores on the hand-scored profile without having to enter each Internalizing and Externalizing item's score.

CONSTRUCTION OF SCALES

Syndrome Scales

The pre-1991 profiles were developed separately for each sex/age group on the TRF. Furthermore, the TRF scales were developed separately from the YSR and CBCL scales. Although the pre-1991 TRF norms for the different sex/age groups were drawn from a single general population sample and the adaptive functioning scales were similar for all sex/age groups, the syndrome scales were developed separately for each group, whether or not similar patterns were found for other groups or on the other instruments.

As the use of the instruments spread and research advanced, closer integration of syndrome scales across sex/age groups and sources of data became more important. For clinical or research reassessment of children as they grow older, for example, it is advantageous to have continuity of scales, while still providing appropriate age norms. For research that involves both sexes, it is helpful to be able to compare them on similar scales. And the limited agreement among informants argues strongly for coordinating multisource data around similar foci.

As outlined in Chapter 3, the 1991 TRF syndrome scales were constructed by deriving *core syndromes* of items that were common to most of the sex/age groups. Furthermore, the core syndromes derived from the TRF, YSR, and CBCL were compared to identify items common to each core syndrome in at least two of the three instruments. The items that were common to a core syndrome in at least two of the three instruments were used to define a *cross-informant syndrome construct*. The items defining the construct represent an hypothetical variable that may underlie the varying manifestations reportable by teachers, youths, and parents. By including on the syndrome scales the items that were specific to the core syndrome derived from a particular type of informant, we retained those aspects of a syndrome that may be evident only to that type of informant. We thus retained variations in problem behavior that may differentiate between the manifestations of particular syndromes in different contexts while advancing the coordination of multiple data sources and highlighting elements of disorders that may be consistent across contexts.

Syndrome Scale Names. The 1991 Withdrawn, Attention Problems, Delinquent Behavior, and Aggressive Behavior syndromes have names quite similar to those on the pre-1991 TRF profile. The 1991 Anxious/Depressed syndrome is the counterpart of the pre-1991 TRF Anxious Syndrome. This syndrome includes items indicative of both anxiety and depression. Some children who score high on the syndrome scale may primarily have anxiety problems that would qualify for a DSM anxiety disorder diagnosis. Other children who score high on the scale may primarily have depressive problems that would qualify for a depressive disorder diagnosis.

Although it is possible to discriminate between feelings of anxiety and feelings of depression, our analyses indicated that these kinds of problems are closely intertwined in children. Many other studies of childhood disorders have also found close associations between problems of anxiety and depression (e.g., Bernstein & Garfinkel, 1986; Cole, 1987; Saylor et al., 1984; Strauss, Last, Hersen, & Kazdin, 1988; Treiber & Mabe, 1987).

The 1991 Social Problems syndrome is a counterpart of the pre-1991 TRF and YSR Unpopular syndrome. The 1991 syndrome designated as Thought Problems is a rough counterpart to the pre-1991 TRF Obsessive-Compulsive scale for boys. It comprises low prevalence problems that were found in a variety of patterns in the pre-1991 analyses.

Internalizing and Externalizing

Like the syndrome scales, the pre-1991 Internalizing and Externalizing groupings were constructed separately for each sex/age group on each instrument. Although there were general similarities among the various versions of the Internalizing and Externalizing groupings, the precise compositions differed because of variations in the syndromes on which they were based. Furthermore, several items were scored on more than one syndrome within the Internalizing or Externalizing grouping, and some items were even scored in both groupings.

For the 1991 profiles, uniform Internalizing and Externalizing groupings were established by averaging the loadings obtained for each of the eight syndromes in separate second-order factor analyses of each sex/age group scored on the TRF, YSR, and CBCL. The three syndromes having the highest mean loadings on the second-order Internalizing factor and the two syndromes having the highest mean loadings on the second-order Externalizing factor were used to define the Internalizing and Externalizing groupings across all sex/age groups on the 1991 TRF, YSR, and CBCL profiles.

Like the cross-informant syndromes, the 1991 Internalizing and Externalizing groupings are quite uniform, although there are also some variations reflecting the items of certain syndromes that are specific to one instrument. Unlike the pre-1991 versions, no items are scored on both Internalizing and Externalizing syndromes, and only one item—*103. Unhappy, sad, or depressed*—is scored on two syndromes (Withdrawn and Anxious/Depressed) within one grouping. However, this item counts only once toward the Internalizing score.

Total Problem Score

Like the pre-1991 TRF total problem score, the 1991 version is the sum of all the problem items on the TRF. If a child obtained a score of 2 on all 120 problem items, the child's total score would be 240.

STATISTICAL RELATIONS BETWEEN PRE-1991 AND 1991 SCALES

Table 8-1 shows Pearson correlations between the raw scores of the pre-1991 and 1991 counterpart scales scored for our 1991 matched referred and nonreferred samples combined. Correlations computed separately for the referred and nonreferred samples did not differ much from those shown in Table 8-1 for the combined samples.

As Table 8-1 shows, most correlations were in the .90s, with the lowest being .83 between the 1991 Social Problems scale and the pre-1991 Unpopular scale for 5- to 11-year-old girls. The high correlations indicate that particular subjects would have very similar rank orders in the distributions of scores on the corresponding pre-1991 and 1991 scales. Correlational analyses and analyses involving the relative magnitude of scores within particular distributions would thus produce similar results using the corresponding pre-1991 and

Table 8-1
Pearson Correlations Between Raw Scores
for 1991 and Pre-1991 Counterpart TRF Scales

Scale	Boys		Girls	
	5-11	12-18	5-11	12-18
$N =$	668	518	758	606
Withdrawn	.98	.95	.96	.96
Anxious/Depressed[a]	.92	.99	.95	.94
Social Problems[b]	.98	.86	.83	.85
Thought Problems[c]	.84	.85	---	---
Attention Problems[d]	.99	.97	.99	.98
Delinquent Behavior	---	---	---	.94
Aggressive Behavior	.99	.99	.99	.99
Internalizing	.96	.97	.95	.96
Externalizing	.93	.95	.93	.95

Note. Subjects were matched referred and nonreferred samples combined. All rs were significant at $p < .0001$. Pre-1991 scales were the closest counterparts of the 1991 scales. Academic, adaptive, and total problem scales are not shown because the pre-1991 and 1991 versions are identical.
[a]Pre-1991 Anxious. [b]Pre-1991 Unpopular. [c]Pre-1991 Obsessive-Compulsive.
[d]Pre-1991 Inattentive.

1991 scales. However, t tests showed significant differences between the absolute magnitude of scores obtained by the same subjects on most of the pre-1991 and 1991 versions of the scales. The significant differences between scale scores reflect the differences between the pre-1991 and 1991 scales in the number and the content of their items. A particular scale score on a pre-1991 scale is thus not necessarily equivalent to the same score on the 1991 counterpart of the scale.

SUMMARY

This chapter summarized differences between the pre-1991 and 1991 TRF scales, the scales having counterparts in the two editions, and correlations between the counterpart scales.

Innovations in the 1991 scales include: Derivation of cross-informant syndrome scales that are common to both sexes and different ages scored on the TRF, YSR, and CBCL; provision of a borderline clinical range on each scale; normalized T scores based on midpoint percentiles; syndrome scales truncated at $T = 50$; easier hand scoring of Internalizing and Externalizing.

Correlations between most pre-1991 and their 1991 counterpart scales were in the .90s, indicating great similarity in the rank ordering of children on the counterpart scales.

The mean scores obtained on most of the pre-1991 scales differed significantly from those obtained on the 1991 scales, owing to differences in the number and content of particular items.   A particular score on a pre-1991 scale is thus not necessarily equivalent to the same score on the 1991 counterpart of the scale.   Nevertheless, the very high correlations between most pre-1991 scales and their 1991 counterparts indicate that correlational analyses and other analyses involving the relative magnitude of scores within particular distributions would produce similar results on the pre-1991 and 1991 scales.

Chapter 9
Practical Applications
of the TRF and Profile

This chapter addresses applications of the TRF to making *practical decisions* about *particular* pupils, groups, programs, policies, etc. Practical applications can be contrasted with *research applications*, discussed in Chapter 10, which aim to establish *principles* that are *generalizable* and *testable*. Designed for both practical and research applications, the TRF is intended to utilize the fruits of research to improve practical assessment and to enrich research by linking it to practical assessment procedures.

The standardized descriptions of pupils' functioning obtained with the TRF provide a common language for practitioners and researchers who can obtain reports from teachers. The TRF is also a key component of multiaxial assessment, for which practical applications are detailed in the *Integrative Guide for the 1991 CBCL/4-18, YSR, and TRF Profiles* (Achenbach, 1991a).

In presenting practical applications, we do not offer clinical "interpretations." Although such interpretations are often sought from assessment instruments, we believe that the meaning and utility of assessment data depend on the situation in which they are to be used. In evaluating children, the skilled practitioner applies knowledge and procedures developed on other cases to obtain a clear picture of the individual case. Our assessment procedures obtain descriptive data in a standardized fashion, aggregated into empirically based scales and normed on large representative samples. These procedures aid the practitioner in identifying specific features of the child as seen by particular informants and compared with normative samples of peers. The profiles show the areas in which the child is in the normal, borderline, or clinical range. The procedures presented in the *Integrative Guide* (Achenbach, 1991a) enable the practitioner to systematically compare data from multiple sources. Hundreds of published studies have reported correlates of the profile scales (Achenbach & Brown, 1991).

Our standardized assessment procedures and their numerous correlates can bring a great deal of accumulated knowledge to bear on the individual case. However, we feel that it would be wrong to provide "canned" interpretations as if they could be mechanically applied to each case. Our procedures can greatly improve the assessment and documentation of children's functioning. Yet, the unique features of each case limit the accuracy with which any procedure can extrapolate clinical interpretations of behavioral/emotional problems to specific cases. Canned interpretations should not be allowed to substitute for the detailed study of the individual case. It is the practitioner who must integrate standardized assessment data with unique information to attain a comprehensive understanding of the case. The essence of clinical creativity is to synthesize diverse procedures and data into an optimal solution for each case.

Responsible practice requires practitioners to test their judgment against various kinds of evidence. The profiles facilitate this process by enabling practitioners to compare informants' descriptions with what similar informants report about normative samples of peers, as well as with the practitioners' own impressions. The profiles also make it possible to compare descriptions of children at different points in time, such as evaluation for special education services, following provision of services, and at follow-up. In the following sections, we provide illustrations and guidelines for using the TRF in various ways when teachers' reports are available.

SCHOOL-BASED SERVICE APPLICATIONS

The most basic function of the TRF and profile is to obtain a teacher's judgment of a pupil in a standardized fashion that facilitates comparisons with normative samples of pupils, with other people's judgments of the same pupil, and with the same teacher's judgments of the pupil at different points in time. The TRF can be used in virtually all school settings. It can be most useful if it is routinely used for all referrals involving behavioral/emotional problems.   Routine use of the TRF provides standardized documentation of problems and adaptive functioning for use in evaluating pupils and for providing a baseline from which to assess change. Figure 9-1 illustrates a typical sequence where the teacher is the first informant.

Teachers' Concerns and Referrals

When teachers become concerned about a pupil's behavior, they may try a variety of remedies, such as increased attention to the pupil, modification of assignments, disciplinary efforts, and contacts with parents. If problems persist, further steps include consulting special education personnel or a school psychologist and encouraging parents to seek help outside the school.

When professional help is sought, teachers' input often consists of referral complaints such as "doesn't pay attention," "hyperactive," "disrupts class," "may have a learning disability," or "not learning." If taken at face value, referral complaints of this sort may unduly narrow the focus of assessment.   A referral complaint of hyperactivity, for example, is often evaluated by having a teacher fill out a checklist designed to assess hyperactivity. If the pupil receives a high score on the checklist, a physician may be asked to prescribe stimulant medication. Without a broader initial assessment, however, it may not be evident that perceived deviance in activity level is

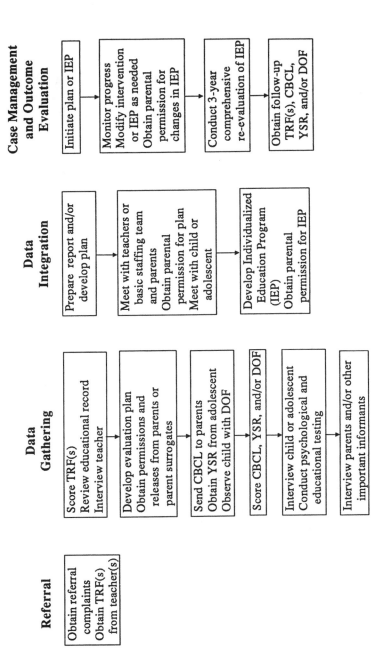

Figure 9-1. Illustrative sequence of empirically based assessment where the teacher is the first informant.

only one facet of problems that are more severe in other areas, such as aggression, anxiety, or unpopularity with peers. The pupil's overactivity—though perhaps real—may also be a by-product of other problems, rather than being the primary problem. On the other hand, the pupil may not really be deviant in the area of the referral complaint, because terms such as "hyperactivity" serve as euphemisms for diverse nuisance behavior.

To obtain from the teacher a more differentiated picture of the pupil's behavior and the degree of deviance in each area, the TRF and profile can be used as soon as a teacher is concerned enough to seek help. Because the TRF does not take long to complete and score, it offers a low-cost basis for comparison with norms for the pupil's age and sex. This may reveal that (a) the deviance is accurately summarized by the teacher's referral complaint; (b) there is significant deviance but it differs from the teacher's referral complaint; or (c) what the teacher reports about the pupil is not really deviant for that pupil's age and sex.

Obtaining a differentiated picture from the teacher is a first step in an evaluation, but it can quickly and efficiently provide a detailed guide for further evaluation and comparison with other data, such as tests of ability, achievement, and perceptual-motor functioning, parents' reports, observations, interviews, and medical exams. In some cases, it may also provide a guide for intervention without much further evaluation. It may be used, for example, to show a teacher that a pupil's problems are within the normal range or are concentrated in different areas than initially assumed. This may help in modifying the teacher's approach to the pupil. The effects of a change in approach can then be re-evaluated by having the teacher fill out the TRF after the new approach has been given a fair trial. Changes in the pupil's behavior—as perceived by the teacher—can be assessed by comparing the second profile with the initial profile.

As an example, Figure 9-2 shows the profile of an 8-year-old third-grader named Todd whose teacher referred him for evaluation of inattention and hyperactivity, which she thought were causing his learning problems. The solid line in Figure 9-2 was derived from the referral TRF completed by Todd's teacher. Todd's scores were at the high end of the normal range on the Attention Problems scale, but above the normal range on the Withdrawn and Social Problems scales. Although the TRF indeed showed a considerable number of attention problems, only the Withdrawn and Social Problems scales showed significant deviance compared to boys of Todd's age.

The profile scored from a CBCL completed by Todd's mother showed deviance mainly on the Anxious/Depressed scale. (Todd's father did not live in the home, but when feasible, CBCLs should be obtained from both parents, so that differences in their perceptions of the child can be identified from their respective profiles.) Todd's mother also reported family problems that were evidently upsetting Todd and for which she agreed to seek counseling for herself and Todd. When the teacher recognized that Todd's learning problems were not due to hyperactivity, she concentrated on developing a warm personal relationship with him and reinforcing positive interactions with other children. A TRF completed five months after the first one yielded the profile shown by the broken line in Figure 9-2.

Comparison of Pupils' Functioning in Different Classes

When pupils have multiple teachers, assessment should take account of possible differences in functioning in different classes and with different teachers. This is easily done by having each of a pupil's teachers fill out a TRF. The resulting profiles can then be compared to identify areas of agreement and disagreement between the different teachers.

Figure 9-3 illustrates profiles scored from TRFs filled out by two teachers of a ninth grade girl named Jean. The

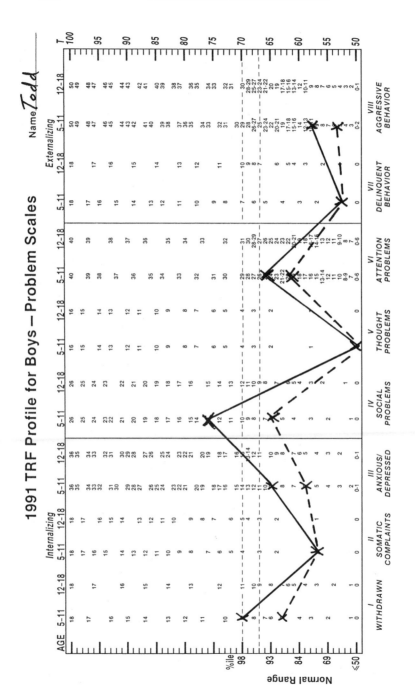

Figure 9-2. TRF profile scored for 8-year-old Todd at referral (solid line) and 5 months later (broken line).

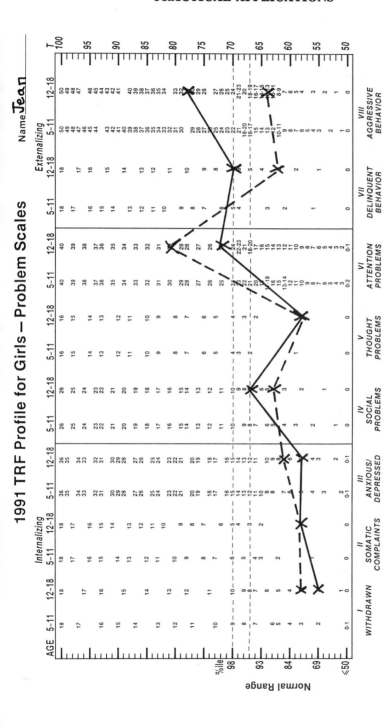

Figure 9-3. Profiles scored from TRFs completed by Jean's English teacher (solid line) and math teacher (broken line).

disagreements should not be viewed as reflecting errors or unreliability, but as information about possible differences in Jean's functioning under different conditions and/or possible differences in the teachers' standards of judgment. Although there was considerable agreement in scores on most scales, the English teacher's TRF (solid line) yielded an especially high score on the Aggressive Behavior scale, whereas the math teacher's TRF (broken line) yielded an especially high score on the Attention Problems scale. Observations in the two classes showed that Jean was in fact aggressive in the English class, where discipline was less strict and several other students were also aggressive. The math class, by contrast, was highly structured, with a strong emphasis on attention to the work. Here, Jean displayed little aggressive behavior, but was noticeably less attentive than most students in the class. The profiles scored from TRFs completed by Jean's science and social studies teachers (not shown) were generally intermediate between those of the math and English teachers.

Since all Jean's TRFs yielded total problem scores above the clinical cutpoint (above $T = 60$) for 12-18-year-old girls, they were unanimous in raising concerns about her. The profiles scored from the four teachers' TRFs also agreed in showing a concentration of problems in the Externalizing area. The contrast between the English and math teachers' profiles suggested that strict classroom discipline and structure could reduce Jean's aggressive behavior, but not eliminate her school problems. Although a tightly structured classroom might thus be a necessary condition for improving her behavior, it was apt to be insufficient without other interventions.

Evaluation of Parents' Concerns

Concern about a pupil's school functioning often originates with parents. Such concerns may be broached as questions about why their child's grades are poor, why disciplinary actions have been taken, or as requests for special services.

When parents approach the school with their concerns, it is important to obtain a picture of the child's behavior from the teacher for comparison with the parents' perceptions. The profile scored from a TRF filled out by the teacher may agree with the parents' impressions, thereby confirming the basis for their concerns. On the other hand, the profile scored from the TRF may differ from the parents' perceptions in several ways: (a) It may show that the parents and teacher perceive different problems; (b) that the teacher does not perceive any significant problems; or (c) that problems blamed by the parents on the school are seen by the teacher as stemming from the child's behavior. A comparison of parent and teacher ratings may reveal more similarities between problems seen at home and school than would be evident from the parents' spontaneous expressions of their concerns. Or it may document major differences between the problems seen at home and school. For example, a child may appear depressed and withdrawn at home but aggressive at school. Further evaluation may also be needed—such as classroom observations, interviews with the child, and testing—to formulate a plan comprehensive enough to take account of the differences between parent and teacher profiles.

Relations to Cognitive Functioning

Because many pupils referred for evaluation are achieving poorly, questions often arise about their cognitive functioning. If tests of ability, achievement, and learning processes are administered, the results can be used in conjunction with the TRF in ways such as the following:

1. If the pupil's cognitive ability is in the normal range, the TRF profile may show deviance that could explain poor academic performance. Deviance on almost any of the problem scales can be associated with poor performance, although the problems scored on the Withdrawn, Anxious/

Depressed, Attention Problems, Delinquent Behavior, and Aggressive Behavior scales may be especially incompatible with good academic performance. The adaptive functioning items of the profile can also contribute to an understanding of poor academic performance in pupils of normal ability. If low TRF ratings of academic performance are corroborated by low achievement test scores despite normal cognitive ability, the teacher's ratings may indicate that the pupil is not working hard or behaving appropriately. In conjunction with behavior problems, this may indicate behavioral and motivational interference with academic learning. If the teacher's ratings for the Working Hard and Behaving Appropriately items are not low, however, and the problem scales do not show deviance that could interfere with learning, a learning disability may be a more likely explanation.

2. If a pupil's cognitive ability is in the retarded range, it should not be surprising if the problem scale scores are high and the adaptive functioning scores are low, compared to normative groups of the same age and sex. High scores on the Social Problems scale for 12-18-year-olds and low scores on the Academic Performance and Learning items, for example, may be direct results of cognitive lags. High scores on other problem scales and a low score on the Happy item, however, may reflect psychological by-products of low ability, rather than low ability per se. Low ability pupils who must compete with pupils of higher ability, for example, may react with problems such as those on the Withdrawn, Anxious/Depressed, and Aggressive Behavior scales. This might argue for protecting the pupil from competition with more able pupils. If the behavior of a low ability pupil is socially inappropriate, as reflected in a low score on the Behaving Appropriately item, this may alienate other pupils, as indicated by a high score on the

Social Problems scale. In such cases, social skills training may be needed to help the pupil get along better with peers.

3. If a pupil is of very low ability (e.g., IQ below 50), self-help skills may require assessment with scales such as the American Association on Mental Deficiency's Adaptive Behavior Scales (Lambert & Windmiller, 1981) or the Vineland Adaptive Behavior Scales (Sparrow, Balla, & Cicchetti, 1984). These scales address self-help and community living skills for which the retarded must often be trained. If the pupil is expected to adapt to mainstream environments, however, the profiles scored from the TRF and CBCL can aid in pinpointing specific kinds of deviance from normal agemates. Although retardation may account for the deviant behavior, altering the behavior may be a prerequisite for successful adaptation. The TRF and CBCL can be filled out again after training to determine whether the pupil's behavior has reached acceptable levels.

Relations to Medical Factors

Physical illness and handicaps can affect pupils' functioning in ways that are assessable with the TRF, which includes an item requesting information on illness, physical disability, and mental handicap. TRF applications in relation to medical factors include the following:

1. A chronic illness, such as diabetes, can create stress that diverts a pupil's attention from school work or leads to interpersonal problems or efforts to overcompensate. Conversely, emotional and behavioral problems can exacerbate such illnesses and interfere with the self-care necessary to control them. Physical handicaps may set limits on pupils' adaptive behavior. Injuries and severe illness, such as cancer, may cause acute disruption that continues to affect a pupil's school functioning long after the initial crisis is over. If a pupil is known to have a medical condition or handicap, it is helpful to obtain both the TRF from the teacher and the CBCL from parents as an aid to determining whether behavior seen in school is so consistent with that seen at home that it may be accounted for by physical abnormalities. Efforts to help should therefor be prosthetic in the sense of adapting the school environment to the pupil's special needs.

2. If a pupil is not known to have a medical condition, certain items on the TRF may suggest the need for medical examination. A pupil who obtains a high score on the Somatic Complaints scale, for example, should be considered for a medical exam. Comparisons with parents' CBCL ratings of the Somatic Complaints scale can therefore be used to identify physical problems that are consistent between home and school and to determine the degree of deviance indicated by the teacher and parent ratings. Aside from physical complaints, items suggesting fatigue, malnutrition, and lethargy, and high scores on the Attention Problems scale may warrant medical evaluations, especially if similar problems are evident in parents' CBCL ratings.

Relations to Specific Environmental Factors

The TRF can reflect problems related to the pupil's home environment, such as the following:

1. Certain behavior that is problematic in the school environment may be typical of a pupil's family or subculture. Aggressive and delinquent behavior, for example, may be disruptive in school but accepted or valued in a pupil's neighborhood. A profile scored from the TRF may correctly show aggressive behavior in the clinical range for a pupil whose siblings show similar behavior and whose family seems unconcerned. This does not necessarily mean that the behavior should be ignored simply because it seems "normal" for that family. If the behavior impedes learning by the pupil or by other pupils, steps must be taken to change it or to overcome its interference with the development of academic skills. The interventions may have to differ, however, from those that are feasible when parents are concerned enough to cooperate in interventions, such as contingency contracting. When parents' aid cannot be enlisted, interventions may have to focus mainly on contingencies in the school setting.

2. Some behaviors that are problematic in the school may reflect a lack of stimulation or opportunity in the pupil's home environment. High scores on the Withdrawn or Social Problems scales, for example, may be due to socially isolated or deprived home environments. In such cases, it may be possible to coordinate school-based efforts with efforts to improve relevant aspects of the home environment.

3. Growing awareness of physical and sexual abuse has given school personnel key roles in detecting, reporting, and ameliorating such abuse. Where a child's poor school performance or deviant behavior on the profile scales cannot be accounted for by other causes, it might be symptomatic of abuse. This would be only one of several possible explanations, but the obligation of school personnel to detect and report abuse adds to the importance of understanding the reasons for deviance found on the profile. This does not necessarily mean that particular scores on the profile are directly diagnostic of abuse, but that they may be clues to be explored in conjunction with other data and hypotheses.

The TRF can also be used to track changes in pupils' reported functioning as the school environment is altered. If pupils have serious enough problems in a regular classroom, for example, they may be assigned to a resource room for part of the school day. By comparing profiles scored from TRFs completed by the regular and resource room teachers, we can determine whether the same problems remain evident in both environments. If so, this would suggest that interventions other than resource room placement should be tried. On the other hand, if TRFs show that pupils have been functioning well in special class settings, TRFs completed by regular class teachers can be used to evaluate functioning during trial mainstream placements. If the profiles show serious problems during the trial placements, further interventions can be designed to overcome the specific problems that prevent successful adaptation to less restrictive environments. The TRF can continue to be used to monitor progress as different interventions and school environments are tried.

COMPREHENSIVE EVALUATION
FOR SPECIAL SERVICES

If it is clear that a child needs special services, it is necessary to base plans on several types of data. Data on cognitive abilities and achievement can be displayed in the form of scores and profiles that compare the child's functioning with that of normative groups of the same age. Similarly, the profiles scored from the TRF and CBCL display the child's competencies and problems as seen by teachers and parents. Whether one person is primarily responsible for a plan or whether it is to be developed by a multidisciplinary team, as with Individualized Education Programs (IEPs), profiles of reported problems provide an explicit basis for (a) exploring discrepancies between the perceptions of different parties; (b) targeting interventions on specific problem areas; and (c) establishing pre-intervention baselines against which to compare changes after a plan has been implemented. The profiles can also aid in determining whether pupils meet special education criteria for categories such as behavioral or social/emotional disturbance, which are often more difficult to apply than those for mental retardation and other handicaps. They can be especially useful for documenting the need for services under Public Law 94-142's (Education of the Handicapped Act, 1977, 1981) category of serious emotional disturbance, for example, which is often difficult to justify without such documentation.

Table 9-1 summarizes applications of the TRF, as well as the CBCL, YSR, and DOF, to P.L. 94-142 determinations of severe emotional disturbance (SED). If referred pupils do not show deviance on any of the scales relevant to the SED criteria, they are unlikely to qualify for SED services under most interpretations of P.L. 94-142. If they do show deviance on scales relevant to the SED criteria and also show evidence of a learning disability, then services should be planned to address both types of problems. It should be remembered that categories such as SED and LD are designed for administrative purposes to determine eligibility for special education services. The categories are not mutually exclusive, and most pupils do not fall neatly into only one category. Instead, pupils who have emotional problems often have learning problems and vice versa. Beside aiding in the administrative determination of eligibility for services, the TRF, CBCL, YSR, and DOF should therefore be used to tailor services to the pupil's specific needs, regardless of the administrative category of services. The following case illustrates the use of the TRF, CBCL, YSR, and DOF in school-based assessment to determine eligibility for services.

Case Example

No single case can illustrate all aspects of assessment relevant to the TRF and CBCL. Pupils, their needs, their families, and their school situations vary in infinite combinations. Elsewhere, we have detailed a conceptual framework for

Table 9-1
Applications of the CBCL, YSR, TRF, and DOF to P.L. 94-142 Criteria for Serious Emotional Disturbance

P.L. 94-142 Components of SED	CBCL	YSR	TRF	DOF
Inability to learn	Attention Problems	Attention Problems	Attention Problems	On task
Inability to build or maintain relationships	Social Problems Withdrawn	Social Problems Withdrawn	Social Problems Withdrawn	Withdrawn-Inattentive
Inappropriate types of behavior or feelings	Aggressive Behavior Thought Problems	Aggressive Behavior Self-Destructive/ Identity Problems[a] Thought Problems	Aggressive Behavior Thought Problems	Attention-Demanding Aggressive Behavior Hyperactive Nervous-Obsessive
General pervasive mood of unhappiness	Anxious/Depressed	Anxious/Depressed	Anxious/Depressed	Depressed
Tendency to develop physical symptoms or fears	Somatic Complaints	Somatic Complaints	Somatic Complaints	—

[a]Scored for boys only. See YSR Manual (Achenbach, 1991c) for details.

Table 9-1 (cont.)

Applications of the CBCL, YSR, TRF, and DOF to P.L. 94-142 Criteria for Serious Emotional Disturbance

P.L. 94-142 Components of SED	CBCL	YSR	TRF	DOF
Schizophrenic	Thought Problems	Thought Problems	Thought Problems	—
Long period of time	Follow-up evaluations	Follow-up evaluations	Follow-up evaluations	Follow-up evaluations
Marked degree	Total, Internalizing, or Externalizing T score ≥ 60	Total, Internalizing, or Externalizing T score ≥ 60	Total, Internalizing, or Externalizing T score ≥ 60	Total score >93rd %ile
	Syndrome T score ≥ 67	Syndrome T score ≥ 67	Syndrome T score ≥ 67	Syndrome >98th %ile
Adversely affects educational performance	School scale T score ≤ 33	—	School performance T score ≤ 40; Adaptive functioning T score ≤ 40	—

empirically based multiaxial assessment (Achenbach, 1985) and have illustrated its application to a wide variety of cases (Achenbach & McConaughy, 1987). Here, we will use a single case to illustrate several facets of assessment relevant to decisions about special services.

Richard, an 11-year-old sixth-grader, had been of concern in the early grades because of problems in learning to read and write, despite IQ test scores in the very superior range. Achievement test scores were far enough below the IQ scores to qualify for services to the learning disabled, but there was no evidence in the test data or a pediatric neurological exam to substantiate a specific learning disability.

By the sixth grade, Richard had progressed in basic skills, but his teachers became concerned about his poor achievement and short attention span. An evaluation included the TRF completed by his teacher, CBCL completed by his mother, the DOF completed by an aide who observed him, and a standard psychometric battery administered by the school psychologist.

Richard's TRF score for school performance was 1.67, which was below the 7th percentile. His total TRF adaptive functioning score was 8, which was also below the 7th percentile. On the CBCL completed by his mother, his score on the Activities scale was well within the normal range, slightly above the 50th percentile, while his score on the Social scale was in the borderline clinical range, at about the 4th percentile. Richard's score of 2 for the School scale was below the 2nd percentile cutpoint of the borderline range. Summed across the Activities, Social, and School scales, Richard's total competence score of 14.5 was in the borderline clinical range.

Richard's total problem scores were 63 on the TRF and 60 on the CBCL. Both scores were in the clinical range and far above the mean of about 22 for nonreferred boys, but were quite typical of referred boys. According to his teacher and parents, Richard was thus seen as having considerably more problems than normative samples of boys and about the same number as many boys who arouse enough concern to be referred for professional help.

Although the teacher's concerns had initially been expressed in terms of poor achievement and attention, the only syndrome scale on which the TRF score exceeded the clinical cutpoint was the Withdrawn scale, with an exceptionally high T score of 91. Consistent with the teacher's concern about poor attention, Richard's second highest score was on the Attention Problems scale. With a T score of 68, it was in the borderline clinical range. Richard's score on the Social Problems scale was also toward the high end of the normal range, but his main problems were clearly concentrated in the area of withdrawal.

Although Richard's mother had not instigated the referral, the problem profile scored from her CBCL showed that she, like the teacher, reported the greatest deviance on the Withdrawn scale (T score = 79), followed by the Social Problems scale (T score = 78). The CBCL profile also reflected deviance on the Attention Problems scale (T score = 73) and borderline deviance on the Thought Problems scale (T score = 70).

The parent and teacher reports were consistent in showing major problems of withdrawal. However, direct observations can provide a check on reports by informants who are personally involved with the pupil. Observations are also mandated by special education regulations in some states and can provide detailed pictures of behavior to be targeted for change. Using the DOF, an aide observed Richard for 10-minute periods on six occasions, including three in the classroom, two during recess, and one in the lunchroom. To obtain a baseline for the typical behavior of boys in Richard's class, the aide also observed two randomly selected boys who sat far away from Richard.

The observer's narrative descriptions and ratings showed behavior distinguishing Richard in the following ways from his classmates: Being preoccupied with fantasy during classwork; often isolating himself from other pupils; making occasional ineffectual efforts to intrude on and get attention from others;

speaking to others in a robot-like way; and making aggressive physical gestures toward others behind their backs. The degree of deviant behavior and its general nature were consistent with the parent and teacher reports, but the observations revealed peculiar and ineffectual aspects of Richard's relations to others that might be difficult to glean from reports by parents and teachers.

The psychometric evaluation yielded a WISC-R Verbal IQ in the superior range, Performance IQ in the average range, and Full Scale IQ in the high average range. All the IQ scores showed a decline of about 17 points from the scores obtained several years earlier. Individual achievement test scores were in the average range, but still far enough below the WISC-R scores to qualify for special educational services. An interview with Richard showed a lack of concern about school achievement and a sense of futility and resignation about relations with others.

In sum, the use of the TRF, CBCL, and DOF in conjunction with standardized tests showed that Richard's school achievement problems were closely entwined with severe problems in interpersonal relations. Although the test scores documented underachievement and an apparent slowing of cognitive development, the TRF and CBCL were able to document specific behavioral/emotional problems warranting help in their own right. The additional details of the behavioral/emotional problems provided by the DOF showed that they might account for Richard's underachievement and that his self-absorption and painful lack of social skills were major obstacles to his adaptive development, including school achievement.

At negligible cost, the parent and teacher ratings and the aide's one hour of observations provided a markedly different picture of Richard's needs than either the referral complaint or the psychometric assessment. Although psychometric assessment is a crucial part of almost all evaluations, analogous data on the pupil's behavioral/emotional functioning outside the test and interview situation are equally important. This what the

TRF, CBCL, YSR, and DOF are designed to provide. We will leave it to you, the reader, to decide the best course of action in Richard's case, but we hope we have persuaded you of the importance and feasibility of including standardized reports from relevant informants in your deliberations.

RE-EVALUATION OF PUPILS

Unless a pupil's functioning is reassessed after a plan is implemented, we cannot know whether the pupil improves, worsens, or remains the same. For some services, such as special education, periodic reassessments are required by law or regulations. Scores on ability and achievement tests provide yardsticks for measuring changes in a pupil's academic functioning from one assessment to another. Profiles scored from the TRF provide similar yardsticks for measuring changes in competencies and problems as perceived by teachers. Because they show how a pupil compares with normative groups of agemates, we can determine whether apparent improvements are sufficient to bring the pupil's functioning into the normal range, or whether the pupil remains outside the normal range in certain areas.

Because they tap multiple areas, the profiles can also show whether there are changes in the patterning of problems or whether certain areas remain unchanged or worsen as other areas improve. Pupils who are treated for hyperactivity, for example, may be found to improve in activity level and attentiveness. If reassessment focused only on these areas, however, worsening in areas such as depression, peer relations, and withdrawal might go undetected. Furthermore, reassessment only of school functioning might neglect a lack of change or worsening elsewhere. CBCLs completed by parents at each reassessment can identify problems outside the school that may require changes in services for a particular pupil. For 11-18-

year-olds, the YSR may also reveal problems not evident to either teachers or parents.

APPLICATIONS IN MENTAL HEALTH CONTEXTS

Referrals

When children's behavioral/emotional problems seem too severe to be handled by regular classroom teachers or the usual special education services, mental health services must be considered, such as outpatient treatment, day programs, hospitalization, and residential placement. It then becomes necessary to determine the most appropriate referral. If public funding is involved, it is also necessary to determine eligibility according to official criteria. The TRF, CBCL, and YSR can be used in determining which type of service is warranted by the severity and kinds of problems seen by the teacher, parents, and pupil. In addition, the TRF, CBCL, YSR, and their scored profiles can be submitted as part of the application for such services, which usually require documentation of the child's functioning.

Use by Mental Health Services

Even when not referred directly by their school, many children seen for mental health services have school problems. As part of clinical evaluations, it is therefore common practice to seek information from the child's school. In such cases, the mental health service can request the child's teacher to fill out the TRF. If the mental health service also requests parents to fill out the CBCL and the child to fill out the YSR, the TRF, CBCL, and YSR profiles can be jointly used as a basis for planning interventions. Thereafter, the TRF, CBCL, and YSR can be readministered periodically to assess changes seen by all three respondents. If schooling is provided as part of a mental health service—such as day, inpatient, and residential treatment programs—TRFs completed by teachers at discharge can be used in preparing the child's return to a regular school.

NEEDS ASSESSMENT AND
PROGRAM ACCOUNTABILITY

Beside the evaluation of individual children, the TRF is designed to address more general questions about groups of children, programs, and the causes and outcomes of childhood disorders. Systematically collecting and analyzing data on groups may sound like research, but these are also necessary steps in determining service needs, even if the findings are never addressed to a research audience.

Needs Assessment

To determine the number of children likely to need special services for behavioral/emotional problems, a survey can be done in which each teacher fills out a TRF on a few randomly selected pupils. If the population to be surveyed is large, such as a state or large school system, an adequate sample can be obtained without burdening teachers by having teachers fill out a TRF for one boy and one girl in their class. When the TRFs have been scored, the proportion of pupils having total scores in the clinical range can be used as a global index of the number likely to need special attention. More differentiated analyses can be done by determining the proportion of deviant pupils for each sex and age, for various localities, types of schools, and types of classes. By analyzing the profile scale scores, the proportion of pupils having particular types of problems can also be determined. If more than the percentage shown in Table 6-3 for nonreferred pupils have scale scores above the clinical cutpoint, this indicates a higher rate of deviance than found in our normative samples.

Program Accountability

To document the kinds of problems referred to particular services and the course of these problems as pupils receive the services, TRFs can be obtained as part of the referral process and then repeated at preselected intervals, such as every 2 months. The distribution of various profile scores can be tabulated for all referred children over a defined period, such as a year, to compare those who do or do not actually receive each available service.

As an example, the distributions of scores at referral can be compared for pupils who are rejected for special services versus those receiving interventions such as behavioral management, counseling, resource room, or self-contained special education. The total problem scores and the scores on each scale can be used to characterize the groups receiving each service. It may be found, for example, that pupils assigned to self-contained special education are distinguished from the other groups by especially high referral scores on the Aggressive Behavior scale, whereas those assigned to resource rooms are distinguished by high scores on the Attention Problems scale. If readministration of the TRF at intervals, such as every 2 months, shows that each group improves significantly in its respective program, the discriminating scale scores can be used to guide the selection of services for children referred thereafter. High scores on the Aggressive Behavior scale might thus be considered one factor favoring self-contained special education, whereas high scores on the Attention Problems scale might favor resource rooms.

Beside documenting the kinds of problems receiving services and the typical course of these problems, the TRF can be used to aid in decisions about changes in services, at both the individual and group level. For example, if no improvements are shown in TRFs filled out periodically on a pupil receiving a service, this could justify changing the service provided to that pupil. To evaluate the effects of particular programs for all the pupils receiving them, TRFs can be filled out when pupils terminate a program and again at follow-up intervals, such as 2, 4, and 6 months. By comparing termination and follow-up scores with those obtained at referral, we can determine whether pupils have improved. If they fail to improve, this would argue for changing the program, changing the assignment of pupils to the program, or developing new programs. If they do improve, it may be worth doing finer-grained analyses by comparing outcomes for pupils differing in initial TRF profile scores or patterns to determine whether some types improve more than others. If so, other services can be used or developed for the kinds of problems that appear not to benefit.

USE OF THE PROFILE OUTSIDE
ITS NORMATIVE AGE RANGE

Because the TRF is the same for ages 5-18, it can be used for initial assessments and reassessments of pupils across these ages. We did not seek normative data for pupils younger than 5, because enrollment in academic school classes is much less common than after 5. Similarly, few youths above age 18 attend regular schools. If children below 5 and youths above 18 are in regular school environments like those in which the profile was normed, TRFs can be scored using the profile norms. However, the greater the difference in age and school environment from the normative groups, the less appropriate the norms will be. Raw total and scale scores can nevertheless remain informative for continuing reassessment of pupils outside the normative range, such as retarded pupils who may remain in special education through the age of 21.

TRAINING OF SCHOOL PERSONNEL

The TRF and profile can aid in training school personnel in a variety of ways, as described below.

Teachers

By having teacher trainees fill out TRFs on their pupils, they can be sensitized to a variety of behavioral/emotional problems that may arise in their classes. As a training exercise, a person knowledgeable about the profile can discuss with teacher trainees the profiles that have been scored from the TRFs they complete. This can sharpen their awareness of the degree and kinds of problems likely to warrant evaluation for special services, as well as the normal range of problems not requiring special services. It can also help them formulate requests for special services in more differentiated and appropriate ways. Although regular classroom teachers would not ordinarily be expected to evaluate profiles, the TRFs completed by trainees can be compared with those completed by supervisory teachers on the same pupils to identify areas in which the trainees may need guidance.

Special Educators

Special education trainees should become familiar enough with standardized assessment of problem behavior to respond appropriately to questions and referrals from regular teachers, as well as to plan and evaluate programs for their own pupils. During training, this can be accomplished by having them fill out the TRF on their own pupils, score the profile, and repeat the process for the same pupils at intervals of about two months. Discussions with supervisors about relations between their teaching efforts, subjective impressions of the pupils, and changes evident in the profile scores can be used to foster more differentiated and objective concepts of pupils' problems. By having trainees review and discuss profiles scored from TRFs completed by other teachers, they can improve their ability to communicate about children and to obtain appropriate information from other people involved with the same children. To take account of children's functioning outside school and learn effective communication with parents, it is also useful for trainees to review profiles scored from parents' CBCLs, to discuss them with parents, and to compare them with profiles scored from TRFs on the same children.

People expecting to become special education supervisors or administrators should have additional experience in using the profiles (*a*) to determine the distribution of problems among pupils referred for special services; (*b*) to guide decisions about assignment to services; and (*c*) to reassess pupils in order to evaluate the services received. Using profiles to document special education caseloads in this way can also improve the ability of future supervisors to plan staff needs, budgets, programs, and collaboration with other types of services for the same pupils, such as welfare and mental health agencies.

School Psychologists

School psychologist trainees are especially apt to need experience with the type of standardized assessment provided by the TRF, its profile, and related instruments. Because school psychologists often bear primary responsibility for assessment of pupils, consultation with other involved parties, and referral for services, they must be able to integrate assessment of cognitive abilities, achievement, behavior, and social/emotional problems. Their training in standardized assessment and statistics should enable them to utilize the various facets of the profile and related instruments more fully than other school personnel.

Because pupils' behavioral/emotional problems are often among the most central issues in referrals to school psychologists, it is helpful to make the TRF a standard part of the referral process, supplemented by the CBCL, DOF, and YSR where appropriate. By obtaining the TRF on all referred pupils, school psychologist trainees can learn the range of variations among pupils' problems, as seen by their teachers. Having TRFs on all referrals also provides a data base from which to do periodic follow-ups, enabling trainees to learn the typical course of pupils they have assessed.

By becoming well-versed in the TRF and routinely obtaining it on all referrals, the school psychologist can establish a uniform reference point for judgment of each new case. The assessment of pupils' school behavior can be enhanced by making direct observations in class, as is now required in some states. Because the DOF includes many of the same items as the TRF, it focuses the observer's attention on problems like those rated by teachers and helps the school psychologist evaluate teachers' judgments of a pupil at first hand, as illustrated by McConaughy (1985).

SUMMARY

The TRF and its profile are designed to obtain teachers' judgments of pupils in a standardized fashion that facilitates comparisons with normative samples of pupils, with other people's judgments of the same pupils, and with judgments of the same pupils at different points in time. Specific applications to individual pupils include the following:

1. Obtaining a differentiated description of the pupil as soon as a teacher is concerned enough to seek help.

2. Comparison of a pupil's functioning in different classes.

3. Evaluation of a pupil's functioning in response to parents' concerns.

4. Comprehensive evaluation of pupils for special services, including IEPs.

5. Determination of eligibility for school-based services.

6. Re-evaluation of pupils after interventions have been implemented.

7. Documentation of children's school functioning for referral to mental health services outside the school.

8. Use by mental health services in clinically evaluating and re-evaluating children, even if the children are not referred by their schools.

Beside applications to individual pupils, the TRF is designed to address questions about groups of children, programs, and the causes and outcomes of disorders, such as the following:

1. *Needs assessments* within particular school systems or geographical areas, which can be done by having teachers in all classes fill out TRFs on randomly selected pupils.

2. *Program accountability*, including documentation of problems among children referred to particular services, aiding decisions about changes in services, and evaluation of program effects.

Educational and clinical diagnostic categories often fail to mesh with each other or with the children to whom they are applied. Such categories are arbitrary conventions rather than direct reflections of the "true" nature of children's problems. The TRF is intended to capture children's problems as they are actually seen, rather than forcing them into predetermined categories, but our empirically-derived syndromes do provide data relevant to clinical diagnoses such as anxiety, depression, attention deficits, and conduct disorders. The Internalizing, Externalizing, and total problem scores provide additional data relevant to criteria for special educational services.

The TRF can aid in the training of teachers, special educators, and school psychologists by helping them form more differentiated pictures of children's behavioral and social/emotional problems, sharpening their awareness of the degree and kinds of problems likely to warrant special help, and focusing their intervention efforts more effectively.

Chapter 10
Research Use of
the TRF and Profile

Chapter 9 outlined some ways in which the TRF can be used for assessment on which to base practical decisions about particular cases and situations. The TRF, its scales, and profile are products of research designed to improve our ways of helping children. Much remains to be learned, however, and the TRF can be used in many ways to expand our knowledge through research.

The *Integrative Guide* (Achenbach, 1991a) focuses on multiaxial aspects of research involving the TRF, CBCL, and YSR. Because agreement between different informants may not be very high, it is desirable to obtain data from multiple sources whenever possible. However, for many purposes, research may center on teachers' reports in particular, or teachers may happen to be the most feasible and appropriate sources of data. This chapter therefore focuses primarily on research use of the TRF, although data from teachers should be viewed as only one component of comprehensive assessment. The topics generally parallel those presented in the *Integrative Guide*, but with variations specific to the TRF.

Use of the TRF is not confined to any single theoretical view, topic, or type of research. Instead, the TRF provides an assessment procedure and data language that can be shared by workers differing in theoretical persuasions and research interests. Furthermore, the TRF can be used in conjunction with many other sources of data, such as tests, self-report questionnaires, interviews, direct observations, parents' ratings, biomedical procedures, and life histories.

Research on a particular type of disorder, such as depression or aggression, typically employs measures specific to that type of disorder. Because the TRF has eight syndrome scales, it can be used to assess disorders corresponding to any of these eight scales. Even if a more specialized procedure is used to assess a particular type of disorder, inclusion of the TRF can reveal problems in other areas that may be equally as important. In research on attention problems, for example, both the TRF and a specialized measure of attention problems may identify pupils who obtain high scores for attention problems. However, the instrument that measures only attention problems will fail to distinguish children whose teachers report only attention problems from children whose teachers would also report significant problems in other areas, if they were asked. The TRF, by contrast, is designed to simultaneously obtain teachers' reports of problems and adaptive functioning in areas beside attention problems. For research on a particular disorder, such as attention problems, the TRF would thus be useful for distinguishing pupils whose teachers report problems only in the area of the target disorder and pupils who present more complex pictures that would be missed if assessment focused only on the target disorder.

This chapter first deals with questions arising in the use of raw scores versus T scores for the TRF scales and in analyzing scores from multiple sex/age groups. Thereafter, it describes applications to research areas including diagnostic and special education classifications, outcomes, services, child abuse, medical conditions, and cross-cultural comparisons. Because creative research blends ideas, opportunities, and methods in new ways, readers will no doubt think of many research possibilities beside those mentioned here. To facilitate access to research possibilities and findings, our *Bibliography of Published Studies Using the Child Behavior and Related Materials* is updated annually. The 1991 edition lists some 200 topics dealt with in over 700 publications (Achenbach & Brown, 1991). Table 10-1 lists examples of research topics for which the TRF has been used in studies listed in the *Bibliography*.

Table 10-1
Examples of Research Topics for which
the TRF has been Used[a]

Abdominal Pain	Inter-Informant Agreement
Adolescence	Learning Disabilities
Aggression	Leukemia
Anger	Low Birthweight
Antisocial Behavior	Maternal Acceptance
Anxiety	Meningitis
Assessment of Psychotherapy	Methylphenidate (Ritalin)
Attention Deficit Disorders	Migraine Headaches
At-Risk Children	Moral Development
Child Abuse and Neglect	Parental Depression
Childhood Depression	Parental Divorce
Competence	Peer Interaction
Conduct Disorders	Psychosocial Development
Cross-Cultural Comparisons with	Public Law 94-142
Dutch, Hispanic & Thai	Short Stature
Children	Social-emotional Disorders
Depression	Sociometric Status
Direct Observations	Stress
Divorce	Superior Intelligence
Drug Treatments	Tourette Syndrome
Family Functioning	Treatment
Father Absence	Visually Handicapped
Hearing Impaired Children	Children

[a]Topics for which studies employing the TRF are listed in the *Bibliography of Published Studies Using the Child Behavior Checklist and Related Materials: 1991 Edition* (Achenbach & Brown, 1991).

USE OF RAW SCORES VERSUS *T* SCORES IN RESEARCH WITH THE TRF

Chapters 2 and 3 described the computation of raw scale scores and the assignment of *T* scores to the TRF scales. The main function of the *T* scores is to facilitate comparisons of the degree of deviance indicated by children's standing on different scales and different instruments. A T score of 70, for example, indicates that a child scored at approximately the 98th percentile of our normative sample for that child's age group and sex. Because the T scores from 50 to 70 were similarly based on percentiles for the syndrome scales of the TRF, a child who obtains a T score of 70 on the TRF Attention Problems scale and 50 on the TRF Somatic Complaints scale is more deviant in reported attention problems than in somatic problems, relative to norms based on teachers' reports.

Suppose that the child who obtained a T score of 70 on the TRF Attention Problems scale obtained a T score of 50 on the CBCL Attention Problems scale. This indicates that the child's teacher reported more severe attention problems, relative to reports by teachers in our normative sample, than did the child's parents, relative to reports by parents in our normative sample.

By being based on percentiles for the normative sample, the T scores provide a convenient way of quickly judging whether a teacher reports relatively many or few competencies and problems, as compared to teachers of nonreferred children. However, because the distributions of scale scores vary among samples, and because of our method for assigning T scores at the extremes of the distributions, the T scores do not provide a perfectly precise and uniform index of deviance. Furthermore, because we truncated the assignment of T scores at the nondeviant end of the syndrome and at both ends of the adaptive functioning scales, raw scores can reflect greater differentiation among pupils than T scores can on these scales. This is not the case for the Internalizing, Externalizing, and total problem scores, however, where the T scores were not truncated.

Statistical Analysis of Scale Scores

For statistical analysis of the adaptive functioning and syndrome scales, it is usually preferable to use the raw scale scores rather than the T scores in order to take account of the full range of variation in these scales. Because T scores were not truncated for the Internalizing, Externalizing, and total problem scores, statistical analyses using the T scores for these scales should yield results similar to those using the raw scores. In any case, the actual distributions of scores to be analyzed should be checked for compatibility with the statistics to be used.   If the obtained distributions depart much from the statistical assumptions, other statistical procedures or transformations of the scores may be needed.

If a researcher wishes to compare a particular sample with our TRF normative samples, the simplest way is to compare the mean and standard deviation of the sample's raw scores with the mean and standard deviation of the raw scores shown in Table 3-4 for the corresponding normative sample. Because any particular research sample is selected differently than our normative sample, the means and standard deviations are likely to differ between the samples. However, the researcher can determine whether the research sample's scores are similar to, much higher, or much lower than those of our normative sample.   Similar comparisons can be made with the scores shown in Appendix B for our referred samples.

The truncation, normalizing transformation, and equal-interval assignment of extreme T scores in our normative samples make direct comparisons with T scores from a particular research sample more tenuous than comparisons of raw scores.   However, if a researcher wishes to describe a sample in terms of our T scores, all the raw scores in the sample should first be individually converted to T scores, as is done by our TRF computer program. The mean and standard deviation of these T scores can then be compared with the mean and standard deviation of the T scores reported for our normative sample in Table 3-4 or clinical sample in Appendix B. The mean and standard deviation of a raw score distribution should *not* be converted directly to the equivalent T scores shown on the TRF profile, because this wrongly assumes that the raw score and T score distributions have identical shapes.

RESEARCH SPANNING MULTIPLE SEX/AGE GROUPS

By using a common set of eight syndrome scales for all versions of the 1991 TRF profiles, we have designed the profiles to facilitate comparisons between both sexes and different ages.   The Internalizing, Externalizing, and total problem scales comprise the same items for all sex/age groups, while the adaptive functioning scales are also uniform for all groups. To take account of sex and age differences in scores, percentiles and T scores were based on separate normative samples of each sex within each age range.   This makes it possible to compare a child's score on any scale with a normative group of the same sex and age range.

If statistical analyses are to be done on samples that include children of both sexes and/or different age ranges, the sex/age differences in scores must be taken into account. On some scales, a particular raw score may represent a different degree of deviance in one sex/age group than in another. For example, a raw score of 29 is in the borderline clinical range on the Aggressive Behavior scale for boys 12-18, but is well above the borderline range for girls 12-18. If we compare the raw scores of two samples that differ greatly in the proportion of boys 12-18 versus girls 12-18, the sample having more boys might appear more deviant. However, because the normative base rate for the problems of the Aggressive Behavior scale is higher for boys than for girls, this would be a misleading conclusion.

To prevent sex/age differences from being confounded with other variables, several options are available. For analyses of the Internalizing, Externalizing, and total problem scores that include multiple sex/age groups, the T scores for the respective sex/age groups can be used. These T scores reflect each subject's deviation from the mean of his/her normative group without losing any of the differentiation that is lost by truncating T scores, as occurs on some of the syndrome and adaptive functioning scales.

For syndrome and adaptive functioning scales that have only one raw score assigned to the truncated T score ($T = 50$ on syndrome scales, $T = 35$ and 65 on adaptive scales), the T scores can be used without any loss of differentiation. For syndrome scales that have multiple raw scores assigned to $T = 50$, the loss of differentiation incurred by using T scores will depend on how many different scores in a research sample would be assigned $T = 50$.

As an example, the Attention Problems scale for boys 5-11 assigns $T = 50$ to raw scores of 0 to 6. If many of the boys in a research sample obtain raw scores of 0 to 6, use of T scores is apt to yield less statistical power than use of raw scores. However, since all scores receiving $T = 50$ are at the low end of the normal range, a researcher may decide that the differences among such scores merely add "noise" to analyses of clinically important variables. The researcher might therefore use T scores to reduce the differentiation among low normal raw scores. On the other hand, if a researcher wishes to preserve all the differentiation in raw scores analyzed for multiple sex/age groups, then the raw scores can be converted to z scores within each of the sex/age groups to be analyzed.

Longitudinal analyses of subjects who are assessed with the TRF before age 12 and again at ages 12-18 can be handled in the same way as just described for analyses that include multiple sex/age groups. That is, the use of T scores will adjust for the differences between norms for the different age ranges. If a researcher wishes to preserve variations within the normal range on the truncated syndrome scales, then the raw scores can be converted to *z* scores within each sex/age range to be analyzed.

In evaluating pupils' behavioral/emotional problems, it is often necessary to fit them into administrative categories of some sort. Within the educational system, the categories usually concern eligibility for particular kinds of services, such as learning disabled or emotionally disturbed. Mental health workers and pediatricians, on the other hand, typically use diagnostic categories, such as the Diagnostic and Statistical Manual (DSM) category of Attention Deficit Hyperactivity Disorder (American Psychiatric Association, 1987). Unfortunately, the lack of correspondence between educational and diagnostic classifications, as well as periodic changes in both types of classification, may make their categories a dubious basis for services.

Cognitive and achievement tests are the main basis for determining eligibility for services to the mentally retarded, learning disabled, and gifted. Other than these, however, few categories rest on specific test-based criteria. Instead, a variety of "soft" data must be integrated to decide whether a child is deviant enough to need special services and to select or justify the most appropriate services. Yet many children do not fit neatly into either educational or diagnostic categories. Even test-based categories such as retardation and learning disability are often complicated by the many borderline cases and the cases that also have behavioral/emotional problems (McConaughy & Ritter, 1985).

To cope with the dilemmas posed by existing administrative classifications, we should first recognize that their categories are arbitrary conventions rather than directly reflecting the "true" nature of children's problems. Classifications impose rules and boundaries that may not fit real children. Because educational systems and mental health services use classification for different purposes, there are always apt to be differences between them, even when knowledge advances enough to produce classifications that more accurately reflect the "true" nature of childhood disorders. The problem, then, is to assess pupils as accurately as possible for the types of decisions that are really needed, without being unduly swayed by administrative criteria.

The TRF, CBCL, DOF, and YSR provide multifaceted descriptions of children from the perspectives of different informants—teachers, parents, observers, and the youngsters themselves. The items are intended to capture descriptive distinctions that can be made without specialized training. The empirically derived syndromes reflect groups of problems that co-occur, as reported by each type of informant. The standardized profiles, in turn, reflect a child's overall pattern of problems as seen by a particular informant and compared to reports by similar informants for normative samples of children.

This form of assessment is intended to capture children's problems as they are actually seen from several perspectives, rather than forcing them into predetermined categories. Nevertheless, the empirically based scales are highly relevant to many classification decisions. If either the total problem score or scores on the syndrome scales are above the clinical cutpoints, this indicates deviance in reported problems. If the Externalizing score is above the cutpoint, this is evidence for problems of an "acting out" nature, whereas an Internalizing score above the cutpoint is evidence for problems of anxiety, depression, withdrawal, and somatic complaints. However, some children are deviant in both these general areas or on the syndromes of the profile that do not belong to these groupings. In such cases, the particular profile pattern can be used as a basis for tailoring services to the child's particular mix of problems and adaptive characteristics.

Descriptive relations between the profile scales and the special education categories of P.L. 94-142 (Education of the Handicapped Act, 1977, 1981) were outlined in Table 9-1. Research is especially needed to test relations between the actual patterns of children's behavioral, emotional, social, and learning problems, on the one hand, and the assignment of children to particular special education services, on the other. Thus, for example, the TRF scores and profile patterns obtained by children who are assigned services for the learning disabled could be compared with those obtained by children who are assigned services for the severely emotionally disturbed. Do the differences between administrative classifications correspond to differences between the children according to teachers' ratings and other assessment data, such as direct observations, interviews, test scores, or self ratings? If assessment data show statistically significant and consistent differences between children assigned to the different services, this would indicate that the assessment procedures could be used to discriminate newly referred children according to whether they most resemble children receiving one type of service versus the other. If children assigned to different special education categories are not initially found to differ, however, this would argue for modifying the administrative classification to conform better to differences among children. A related question is whether many children who are deviant on the TRF and other empirically based assessment procedures fail to qualify under the prevailing administrative criteria. If this were found to be the case, then new criteria should be developed to take account of these children's needs.

OUTCOME RESEARCH

If we knew the typical outcomes for various kinds of childhood problems following no intervention and following each of several intervention options, we would be in a much better position to make decisions about individual cases. Furthermore, if types of problems were identified that typically had poor outcomes following all available interventions as well as following no intervention, these types of problems should receive high priority for research designed to improve interventions. Because teachers are usually involved in the assessment of children for school-based interventions, their reports are a prime source of baseline data with which to compare outcomes. If we find that particular TRF scores or profile patterns are typically followed by much worse outcomes than other scores or patterns, then new cases manifesting the prognosticators of poor outcomes can be selected for research efforts to improve their outcomes. Other variables, such as parent-, observer-, and self-ratings, interview data, family constellation, cognitive measures, achievement tests, and biomedical conditions, might also be found to augment predictions of outcomes. These variables could then be used in conjunction with the TRF to identify pupils expected to have poor outcomes and to develop better ways of helping them.

Just as additional variables may augment prediction of outcomes from initial characteristics, the outcomes themselves should be evaluated using criteria in addition to the TRF whenever possible. The additional criteria could include parent-, observer-, and self-ratings obtainable with the CBCL, DOF, and YSR, cognitive functioning, new problems, referral for various services, etc.

Beside testing predictions of outcomes from child-related variables, outcome research can be useful for determining the relative risk rates for children thought to be predisposed to poor outcomes by certain identifiable background conditions. Children whose family members are alcoholic, schizophrenic, or depressed, for example, are thought to be at elevated risk for behavioral/emotional problems. To determine whether such children have elevated rates of problems in general or the specific problems tapped by particular syndrome scales, TRFs can be compared from teachers of children in each of several risk groups and children not having any of the risk factors. Teachers' ratings would be especially valuable if teachers are unaware of the differences in risk factors. In a study by Richters and Pellegrini (1989), for example, TRF problem scores were significantly higher for children of depressed mothers than for children of mothers with no history of depression. Teachers' TRF ratings also showed similar levels of agreement with CBCL ratings by depressed mothers during depressive episodes, ratings by depressed mothers in remission, and ratings by nondepressed control mothers.

SERVICES RESEARCH

Experimental Intervention Studies

If outcome research identifies pupil characteristics that predict poor outcomes, this argues for active efforts to improve outcomes for these cases. The most rigorous way to determine whether a particular intervention can improve outcomes is to experimentally manipulate the intervention conditions. Experimental studies require a large enough supply of appropriate cases to be assigned to different experimental conditions, such as by randomized assignment to Intervention A versus Intervention B versus no intervention. For some types of interventions, such as drugs or contingency manipulations designed to alter specific behaviors, it may be possible to test each intervention with the same subjects receiving both interventions in counterbalanced sequences, such as ABAB and BABA.

To warrant the effort and cost of experimental intervention studies, candidate subjects must be assessed in a uniform fashion to identify those who have the target characteristics and to exclude those who do not. If deviant scores on particular TRF scales were previously found to predict poor outcomes, then these scores could be used to select subjects for an intervention study. Subjects who were not deviant on the target scales or who were deviant on additional scales could be excluded from the study. Moreover, the initial TRF scores can be used as a baseline against which to measure change by readministering the TRF again after the experimental conditions and comparing pre- versus post-intervention scores for subjects receiving the different conditions. Other measures, such as direct observations, parent-reports, self-reports, interviews, and tests could also be used to evaluate the intervention effects. The *Integrative Guide* (Achenbach, 1991a) presents further details of experimental intervention designs using multiple pre- and post-intervention measures.

Operations Research

As discussed in Chapter 9, the TRF can be applied to planning and program accountability within a particular school system. Whether the aim is to make practical decisions about a particular system or to identify general phenomena and principles, a research perspective can aid in promoting rigorous data collection, analysis, and conclusions. Rigorous documentation of the functioning of systems is known as *operations research*, which has been defined as "the application of scientific methods, techniques, and tools to problems involving the operations of a system so as to provide those in control of the operations with optimum solutions to the problems" (Churchman, Ackoff, & Arnoff, 1957, pp. 8-9).

TRF item scores, scale scores, and profile patterns can be used to document the kinds of problems seen in particular school services and the relations of these problems to other variables, such as sex, age, SES, ability levels, etc. The TRF scores and profile patterns can also be used to classify pupils as they enter, move through, and leave special services. By comparing the type, duration, and outcome of services for pupils who differ in initial TRF scores and patterns, we can determine whether services, costs, and outcomes vary according to the problems reported by the children's teachers.

Another form of operations research involves cross-referencing between empirically based procedures, such as the TRF, and administrative classifications such as Public Law 94-142 categories for special education. Operations research can be designed to determine how consistently the administrative classifications relate to the empirically based measures. For this type of research to be worthwhile, however, it is important to demonstrate that the administrative classifications are reliable enough to attain significant associations with the TRF scores. If the administrative classifications are unreliable, this will preclude finding relations to measures such as the TRF.

RESEARCH ON CHILD ABUSE

School personnel are expected to detect and report child abuse. When abuse has been detected, assessment of the child is often needed for forensic purposes and as a basis for recommendations and interventions. The TRF can be useful in several ways related to abuse. For children experiencing abuse from family members, teachers may be a better source of data than parents, who may attempt to minimize or exaggerate the effects of abuse.

As with other risk factors, it is important for research on abuse to take account of multiple possibilities. Rather than merely searching for unique symptoms of abuse, for example, it is important to test whether abuse exacerbates pre-existing problems or has different effects on different children. For studies of children known to be abused, comparisons with clinical samples of nonabused children are needed to identify ways in which particular subgroups of abused children may differ from other referred children. The TRF can also be used in conjunction with other assessment procedures to study the progress of abused children receiving different intervention conditions, such as individual therapy, family therapy, or foster placement.

RESEARCH ON MEDICAL CONDITIONS

Certain behavioral/emotional problems may accompany particular medical conditions. In some cases, a medical condition or a medical treatment may specifically cause problems that are evident to teachers, such as inattention, motor tics, depression, lethargy, or overactivity. In other cases, a medical condition may cause stress that raises the risk of behavioral/emotional problems. To determine whether particular behavioral/emotional problems tend to accompany particular medical conditions, the TRF can be used to compare pupils having each medical condition with pupils having other medical conditions and with physically healthy pupils. The comparisons between pupils having different medical conditions are helpful for avoiding erroneous attributions of elevated rates of problems to a particular condition, when they may actually accompany multiple conditions.

The TRF can be used as an outcome measure in interventions aimed at reducing behavioral/emotional problems associated with medical conditions. Afflicted pupils can be assessed with the TRF before and after receiving a particular intervention versus a control condition to determine whether the pupils have fewer behavioral/emotional problems after the intervention than after the control condition. Because teachers are usually less involved with children's medical conditions and treatment, their ratings may be less vulnerable to the stress of having an ill child than are ratings by parents.

CROSS-CULTURAL RESEARCH

To advance the study of child psychopathology, it is important to calibrate assessment procedures across different countries and cultures. If similar procedures produce similar results in different cultures, this supports the cross-cultural robustness of the findings and the possibilities for integrating results from the different cultures. If different results are obtained from different cultures, by contrast, the findings may provide clues as to causal factors related to the cultural differences.

The TRF is being increasingly used in studies outside the United States, including Australia (Sawyer, Crettenden, & Toogood, 1986), Canada (Beitchman, Nair, Clegg, Ferguson, & Patel, 1986), China (Li, Su, Townes, & Varley, 1989), Holland (Verhulst & Akkerhuis, 1989), Puerto Rico (Achenbach et al., 1990), Thailand (Weisz et al., 1989), and Turkey (Akkok & Askar, 1989). At this writing, we know of translations of the TRF or our related forms into the 33 languages listed in Table 10-2.

Table 10-2
Translations of the TRF, CBCL, and/or YSR

Afrikaans	Korean
Amharic	Norwegian
(Ethiopia)	Papiamento-Aruba
Arabic	Papiamento-Curacao
Bengali	Portuguese
Cambodian	Portuguese Creole
Chinese	Russian
Dutch	Samy
Finnish	(Norwegian Laplanders)
French	Sotho
(Canadian & Parisian)	(South Africa)
German	Spanish
Greek	(Argentina, Chicano,
Haitian Creole	Chile, Puerto Rico,
Hebrew	Spain, & others)
Hindi	Swedish
Hungarian	Thai
Icelandic	Turkish
Italian	Vietnamese
Japanese	Zulu

SUMMARY

The TRF, its scales, and profile are products of research, and they can be used to expand our knowledge through research. Like practical applications, research should use multiple sources of data about children's functioning. Teachers' reports are essential for most research on children's behavior in school and are also valuable for providing additional perspectives on children studied in other contexts. Because the TRF is not confined to a single theoretical viewpoint, it can be applied to research concerning many types of questions, theories, and other assessment procedures.

This chapter presented reasons for using raw scores rather than T scores for most statistical purposes and outlined ways of spanning multiple sex/age groups in research with the TRF. It also addressed applications to research areas including diagnostic and special education classifications, outcome research, services research, child abuse, medical conditions, and cross-cultural research.

Chapter 11
Assessment Materials
Related to the TRF

Teachers' reports are clearly an important source of assessment date for children attending school. However, the moderate correlations between teachers' reports and reports by others (Achenbach et al., 1987) indicate that multiple sources of data are needed for comprehensive assessment. The CBCL/4-18 obtains parents' reports and the YSR obtains self-reports in formats that facilitate comparisons among the three instruments. These three instruments have 89 similar problem items in common, but each instrument also has additional items geared to the type of informant for whom the instrument is designed.

The *Integrative Guide for the 1991 CBCL/4-18, YSR, and TRF Profiles* (Achenbach, 1991a) presents the procedures used to develop the eight 1991 syndrome scales common to these three instruments. The *Guide* describes a microcomputer program that is available for entering, scoring, and comparing data from all three instruments. Separate Manuals are available that present detailed information on the development and use of the CBCL (Achenbach, 1991b) and YSR (Achenbach, 1991c).

In the *Integrative Guide*, findings on associations between the TRF, CBCL, and YSR have been presented to facilitate the general coordination of cross-informant data in assessment for clinical and research purposes. Here we will focus on the degree of association between TRF scores obtained from teachers, CBCL scores obtained from parents, and YSR scores obtained from adolescents. The correlations are between the corresponding scales of the different instruments, but the items of the corresponding scales are not necessarily identical. As detailed in Chapter 3, the scales for the cross-informant syndromes include some items that are specific to a particular instrument. In addition, the wording of counterpart items varies among the instruments to make them appropriate for the particular informants.

To enable us to compare data on precisely the same subjects for the different combinations of informants, Dr. Michael Sawyer has graciously permitted us to use his data from a general population sample participating in a longitudinal study in Adelaide, Australia (Sawyer, 1990). Because subjects were not screened out according to referral status, a few of the subjects had been referred for mental health services, but most had not. A particular strength of this sample is that it provides independent ratings by teachers, fathers, mothers, and youths on the same subjects. The subjects were 183 boys and 179 girls aged 11 to 16. Although the findings may not be precisely generalizable to the United States or other countries, the standard American versions of the TRF, CBCL, and YSR were used.

Table 11-1 presents Pearson correlations of TRF ratings with ratings by fathers, mothers, boys, and girls. The *r*s of ratings of Academic Performance were somewhat higher for teachers x parents than for teachers x youths, but they did not differ much according to the sex of the parent or sex of the youth. The mean *r*s for the problem scores were somewhat higher for boys than girls in all combinations of informants, ranging from .48 to .58 for boys and .35 to .46 for girls. The differences between correlations were not significant in this sample, although the tendencies for cross-informant correlations to be somewhat higher for boys than girls on our measures were significant for some comparisons in larger samples (Achenbach, 1991a).

Of the eight syndromes common to the three instruments, the *r*s for the Social Problems syndrome were consistently

Table 11-1
Correlations of TRF Ratings with CBCL
and YSR Ratings

Scale	Correlations for 183 Boys			Correlations for 179 Girls			Mean r
	Fathers	Mothers	Self	Fathers	Mothers	Self	
Academic Performance	.69	.62	.51	.61	.61	.55	.60
Withdrawn	.56	.49	.50	.41	.50	.36	.47
Somatic Complaints	.16	.20	.15	.21	.26	.20	.20
Anxious/Depressed	.37	.48	.46	.33	.43	.26	.39
Social Problems	.70	.73	.60	.57	.57	.55	.63
Thought Problems	.29	.41	.30	(.14)	.39	.20	.29
Attention Problems	.70	.70	.53	.48	.49	.41	.56
Delinquent Behavior	.71	.71	.55	.55	.55	.45	.60
Aggressive Behavior	.59	.62	.52	.38	.41	.33	.48
Internalizing	.48	.50	.51	.31	.48	.31	.44
Externalizing	.65	.66	.55	.45	.48	.39	.54
Total Problems	.66	.69	.55	.42	.50	.38	.54
Mean r	.55	.58	.48	.39	.46	.35	

Note. All rs were significant at $p < .05$ except the one in parentheses. Data were from an Australian general population sample participating in a longitudinal study by Sawyer (1990).

among the highest for all combinations of raters and yielded the highest mean *r* across all combinations of informants. Where TRF ratings are concerned, the Social Problems syndrome may thus tap an area of particular consistency among informants' perceptions of young adolescents.

The mean *r*s shown in Table 11-1 were considerably higher than the mean *r* of .27 between teacher- and parent-reports and .20 between teacher- and self-reports obtained in our meta-analyses of many studies using different instruments (Achenbach et al., 1987). The lower correlations obtained in the meta-analyses might be partly accounted for by the wider age range included there. That is, teachers might agree less with parent- and self-reports for both younger and older pupils than with the 11- to 16-year-olds in Sawyer's (1990) sample analyzed here. Higher cross-informant correlations than in our meta-analyses have also been obtained when the TRF was used in our normative sample (Achenbach, 1991a).

SUMMARY

This chapter presented correlations between corresponding scales of the TRF, CBCL, and YSR, separately for boys and girls. The correlations between TRF problem scores and the other instruments tended to be somewhat larger for boys than girls, but the difference was not significant. The cross-informant correlations were considerably higher than the correlations obtained with teacher-reports obtained in meta-analyses of studies using many different instruments. Agreement among the TRF, CBCL, and YSR was especially good on the Social Problems syndrome, where the mean *r* was .63 across all combinations of raters.

Chapter 12
Answers to Commonly Asked Questions

This chapter answers questions that may arise about the TRF and the profile on which it is scored. Although earlier sections of the Manual addressed many of these questions, we list them here to provide explicit answers, supplemented by references to more detailed information where relevant. The questions are grouped according to whether they refer mainly to the TRF itself, to scoring the TRF, or to the profile on which the scores are displayed. If you have a question that is not found under one heading, look under the other headings as well. The Table of Contents and Index may also help you find answers to questions not listed here. For questions about relations between the TRF and the 1991 CBCL/4-18 and YSR, consult the *Integrative Guide for the 1991 CBCL/4-18, YSR, and TRF Profiles* (Achenbach, 1991a).

QUESTIONS ABOUT THE TRF

1. How does the 1991 TRF differ from previous editions of the TRF?

Answer: Small changes in wording have been made to clarify a few items. The largest changes are in Item *42* (page 3), where the wording has been changed to *Would rather be alone than with others*, from *Likes to be alone*, and Item *56a* (page 3), where *(not headaches)* has been added to clarify that headaches should not be included with "aches or pains." These changes do not affect scoring. The 1991 TRF can be scored on the pre-1991 profile. Conversely, the pre-1991 TRF can be scored on the 1991 profile.

2. Why is the TRF said to have 118 problem items, when the item numbers only go to 113?

Answer: Item *56* includes seven specific physical complaints designated as *a* through *g*. Combined with the remaining 111 specifically stated problems, this sums to 118 items. In addition, Item *56h* provides space for teachers to enter any physical problems not otherwise listed, and Item *113* provides three spaces for teachers to add additional problems of any sort. Total problem scores are computed as the sum of 1s and 2s for the 118 specific problem items + Item *56h* + the highest score the respondent gives to any additional problems written in for Item *113*. If a 2 is scored for all 118 items, *56h,* and *113,* the total score would be 240.

3. Can the TRF be filled out by people other than teachers?

Answer: The TRF is designed to record pupils' functioning as seen by their classroom teachers. If another person, such as a guidance counselor or school administrator, is familiar with a pupil's classroom functioning or collates TRF data from a pupil's teacher(s), such a person could also fill out the TRF. This may be necessary if no teacher knows the pupil well. However, because the normative data were obtained directly from teachers, and teachers are typically in the best position to observe the characteristics assessed by the TRF, teachers are usually the most appropriate respondents.

4. What if a child has a tutor or is in a special class or residential treatment setting?

Answer: If a child is not in a teaching situation with other pupils, many of the TRF items concerning peer interactions and classroom behavior will not be scorable. This will limit comparability with the normative groups on the scales of the profile. However, if pupils are taught together in special educational or residential treatment settings, there is usually enough opportunity for peer interaction to make the TRF and profile fully relevant.

5. If a pupil is in a special class or is known to be handicapped, should a teacher still compare him/her to "typical" pupils?

Answer: Because the profile is designed to compare individual pupils to normative samples of pupils, the teacher should base ratings on what is expected of "typical" pupils in regular classes. It should not be surprising if special class and handicapped children obtain low scores for adaptive functioning and high scores on the problem scales compared to normative groups. However, the specific areas of deviance from normative groups are often important for planning a pupil's program, evaluating progress, and determining placements, such as mainstreaming versus special classes.

6. What if a pupil has several teachers?

Answer: In junior and senior high schools, as well as departmentalized elementary schools, pupils may not have a single teacher who is familiar with the full range of their functioning. This presents opportunities to compare a pupil's functioning in different classes by obtaining TRFs from each of the relevant teachers. The profiles scored from each teacher's TRF can be compared to identify areas of similarity and difference. Differences between the pictures obtained from different teachers can be explored to determine the reasons why perceptions of the pupil's functioning vary from one class to another. Scale scores obtained from TRFs completed by several teachers can also be averaged to form a composite profile that summarizes a pupil's functioning across classes. For research purposes, these composite profiles can be used in analyses of groups of subjects rather than using multiple profiles for each subject.

7. What if teachers say they don't know enough about a pupil to score certain items?

Answer: If a pupil has been in a teacher's class for at least two months, the teacher should be encouraged to score all items as completely as possible, even if guessing is necessary. On the problem items (pages 3-4), it can be pointed out that a score of 0 does not require complete certainty that the problem does not occur, but merely that the teacher does not know it occurs—i.e., the instructions state: *0 = Not True (as far as you know)*. If more than 8 problem items are left blank (not counting Items *56h* and *113*), the problem scale scores will not be fully comparable to those for our normative groups, unless it is clear that the respondent intends the blank items to be scored 0. However, because teachers sometimes leave Items *56a-g* blank if they have seen no evidence for physical problems without known medical cause, these items can be scored 0 if the teacher has left them blank. Appendix A provides detailed scoring instructions.

8. Don't certain items involve subjective judgments, such as *35. Feels worthless or inferior* and *52. Feels too guilty*?

Answer: Subjectivity is involved in all ratings of any person by another person. The TRF is designed to obtain judgments of the type that many teachers make of their pupils, although it is recognized that some items involve more subjectivity than others. Leaving out these items, however, would limit the range of assessable problems to the most obvious externalizing behaviors.

9. Can the TRF be used for ages below 5 and over 18?

Answer: We designed the TRF for ages 5 through 18, because these are the ages when the largest proportion of youngsters attend academically oriented programs. Prior to the age of 5, school experiences are more variable and less academically oriented than after 5. The few youths who remain in school after age 18 are apt to be quite atypical. Nevertheless, as long as the lack of age-specific norms is recognized, the TRF can be used for 4-year-olds and for 19-year-olds who are in regular school programs. The more the age and type of school setting deviate from those for which norms were constructed, however, the more caution is needed in using the standard scores, percentiles, and cutpoints.

10. Page 3 of the TRF instructs the respondent to base ratings on the previous 2 months. Can this period be changed?

Answer: The 2-month period was selected as sufficient for pupils' behavior to stabilize in a new class situation and for teachers to become well enough acquainted with their pupils to provide satisfactory ratings. Thus, for a school year beginning in September, teachers would not usually be expected to complete the TRF before the end of October. However, in situations where teachers already know their pupils well, it may be possible to base ratings on shorter intervals, especially where the effects of interventions are being evaluated to see whether the teacher perceives changes in a pupil's functioning. It should be kept in mind, nevertheless, that reassessments over brief periods may be more vulnerable to random or short-lived fluctuations of behavior.

11. Is there a short form of the TRF that takes less time to complete?

Answer: There is no short form as such. However, the time can be reduced by omitting information on the parents' occupations and all the items that are not scored on the profile (Items I-VI and IX-X, and the open-ended items on page 2). If the ratings of adaptive functioning are not needed, the problem portion can be completed alone. Although the list of problems looks long, it can usually be completed in 8-10 minutes. Because each scale's standard scores assume that the respondent considers all the items of the scale, it would not make sense to abbreviate the TRF any further.

12. Has the TRF been translated into other languages?

Answer: At this writing, we know of translations of our forms into the 33 languages listed in Table 10-2. For the current status of TRF translations into a particular language, write to Dr. Achenbach.

SCORING THE TRF

Appendix A contains detailed scoring instructions, including criteria for items the respondent is asked to describe.

1. What if the respondent scores two different items for exactly the same behavior?

Answer: Score only the item that most specifically describes the behavior. For example, if the respondent circled a 2 for Item *1. Acts too young for age* and also circled a 2 for Item *84. Strange behavior*, describing the behavior as "acts very babyish," only Item *1* should be counted.

2. What if the respondent circles two scores for a particular item or otherwise indicates that the item is true of the pupil but does not clearly indicate a score of 1 or 2?

Answer: Score the item 1.

3. On Item *113*. *Please write in any problems the pupil has that were not listed above*, what if a respondent describes behavior that is specified elsewhere on the problem list?

Answer: Score the problem only where it is most precisely specified on the problem list, whether or not the respondent has scored it there as well as in Item *113*. For example, if the respondent wrote "eats pieces of paper," and scored it 2 for Item *113*, only Item *28*. *Eats things that are not food* should be scored 2, rather than Item *113*, whether or not the respondent had also scored Item *28*.

4. How is Item 113 figured in the total score?

Answer: If the respondent enters on Item *113* a problem that is not clearly covered by another item, obtain the total problem score by adding the 1 or 2 scored by the respondent to the sum of 1s and 2s for all other items. If the respondent enters more than one additional problem, count only the one having the highest score. Thus, if a respondent scored one additional problem 1 and another problem 2, add 2 to the total score. (Adding a maximum of 2 points for Item *113* and 2 for *56h* is intended to limit the amount of variance contributed by items that are not stated for other teachers to rate.)

5. Should TRFs that have many unanswered items be scored?

Answer: The scoring instructions (Appendix A) give rules for dealing with unanswered items. In brief, if any of the four adaptive characteristics (Items *VIII.1-4*) is omitted, do not compute the sum of the remaining adaptive characteristics. If Items *56a-56g* are blank, these can be scored as zero. If more than 8 other problem items are left blank (excluding Items *56h* and *113*), do not compute problem scale scores or total scores, unless it is clear that the respondent intended the blanks to be zeroes.

6. How is the total problem score used?

Answer: This score provides a global index of the pupil's problems, as seen by the respondent. We have found that T score = 60 provides a good cutpoint for discriminating between referred and nonreferred children. The total problem score can also be used as a basis for comparing problems in different groups and for assessing change as a function of time or intervention.

1991 TRF PROFILE

1. How does the 1991 profile differ from the previous edition?

Answer: Chapters 2 and 3 describe the 1991 profile scales in detail. Briefly, the main innovations include *(a)* scoring children in terms of the same eight syndromes and the same Internalizing and Externalizing groupings of syndromes for all sex/age groups on the TRF and also on the CBCL/4-18 and YSR; *(b)* use of a new national sample to norm the profiles of all three instruments; *(c)* inclusion of ages 5 and 17-18 in the norms; *(d)* changes in normative age ranges to 5-11 and 12-18 years; *(e)* extension of syndrome T scores down to 50; *(f)* demarcation of a borderline clinical range; and *(g)* easier computation of Internalizing and Externalizing scores on the hand-scored profile.

2. How can hand scoring be made quicker and easier?

Answer: We offer scoring templates that fit over the TRF and indicate the scales on which each item is scored. The 1991 TRF profile is easier than the previous edition to score by hand, because the same templates are used for all four sex/age groups. Furthermore, to compute Internalizing and External-izing scores, the individual items no longer need to be entered and summed. Instead, the syndrome scores are merely summed and the one redundant item is subtracted. The time taken to score profiles usually decreases with experience. Certain scores can be omitted if you do not need them, such as the Internaliz-ing and Externalizing scores. If we grouped behavior problem items on the TRF according to their profile scales, this might make scoring easier. However, it could create a halo effect on the respondent's ratings. We recommend computer scoring whenever feasible, but we welcome suggestions for making hand scoring easier. Contact Dr. Achenbach for information on computer scoring programs.

3. Why are some problem items included on more than one profile scale?

Answer: As explained in Chapter 3, problem items are included on each syndrome for which they met criteria for the cross-informant syndrome constructs. In addition, a few items that met criteria for the TRF core syndromes are included in TRF versions of the syndrome scales. Five items are included in more than one 1991 TRF syndrome scale. Of these, Item *103. Unhappy, sad, or depressed*, is included on two Internaliz-ing scales, but it is counted only once toward the Internalizing score. No item of the Externalizing scales is included on more than one scale.

4. Why are there no norms for the "Other Problems"?

Answer: The "Other Problems" on each profile do not form a scale but are merely the items that were too uncommon to be included in the derivation of syndromes or did not qualify for the syndrome scales. There are thus no associations among them to warrant treating them as a scale. However, they are included in the total problem score.

5. Should raw scores or T scores be used to report results?

Answer: Chapter 10 discusses the different uses of raw scores and T scores in detail.

6. Does a high score on the Delinquent Behavior scale mean that a child is a juvenile delinquent?

Answer: The names of the scales are mainly intended to summarize the content of the scales. The term "Delinquent Behavior" literally refers to "conduct that is out of accord with accepted behavior or law" and "offending by neglect or violation of duty or law" (Mish, 1988, p. 336). Although some items of the Delinquent Behavior syndrome, such as stealing, are illegal, a high score on the scale for this syndrome does not necessarily mean that a child has broken laws or will be adjudicated as a delinquent. Instead, it means that the child is reported to engage in more behaviors of the empirically derived Delinquent Behavior syndrome than are reported for normative samples of peers. Similarly, the labels for other syndromes provide summary descriptions for the kinds of problems included in the syndromes, rather than being directly equivalent to any administrative or diagnostic category.

7. Should extremely low scores on any problem scales be considered deviant?

Answer: No, because extremely low scores merely reflect the absence of reported problems. As explained in Chapter 3, the profile compresses the low end of the problem scales, so that a T score of 50 is the minimum obtainable on any scale.

However, most pupils have at least some problems. The mean problem scores for nonreferred pupils in our normative samples ranged from 15.6 for 12-18-year-old girls to 23.8 for 12-18-year-old boys (see Table 3-4).

8. Should there be separate norms for pupils of different socioeconomic or ethnic groups?

Answer: Chapter 6 shows that socioeconomic and ethnic differences are generally too small to warrant separate norms.

9. If a pupil is in the 5-11 age group at the initial rating and is 12-18 at a later rating, which profile should be used?

Answer: The 1991 scales are based on the same items for both age groups. These scales can be used to compare TRFs filled out at different ages merely by using the T scores appropriate for the pupil's age at each rating. If a precise comparison using the same T scores is desired for pupils who were age 11 at the first rating and age 12 at the second, the age 12 T scores can be used at both points. (Chapter 10 provides further information on scoring across age periods.)

10. How are interpretations of the profile made?

Answer: The profile is intended as a standardized description of behavior, as seen by the person filling out the TRF and compared to reports by teachers of pupils of the same age and sex as the subject. As such, it is to be integrated with everything else that is known about the pupil, instead of being viewed as a key to hidden entities, as projective tests sometimes are. Rather than being "interpreted," the information from the profile should be integrated with other data to provide a picture of the pupil consisting partly of the pupil's standing on dimensions assessable for pupils in general, such as those of the CBCL, YSR, DOF, and cognitive measures, and partly of unique characteristics of the pupil. Specific guidelines and illustrations are provided in Chapter 9.

9. Is there a "lie" scale for the profile?

Answer: Deliberate lying is only one factor that can lead to excessively low or high scores, depending on whether the informant denies or exaggerates problems. Social desirability sets, over-scrupulousness, and misunderstandings can also affect ratings. Because of the variety of possible influences and our desire to restrict the TRF to items that are meaningful in themselves, we did not add items designed to detect the various kinds of influences. Instead, we stress that profile scores should never be used to make judgments in isolation from other information about the pupil and the informant; the scores should always be compared with other data to identify major distortions and to determine the possible reason for distortions. Extremely low or high total scores for problems or adaptive functioning should always be followed up to determine whether they accurately reflect the informant's view of the pupil, and, if so, whether this view differs markedly from other people's view of the pupil. Although teachers are not apt to deliberately distort their responses, the following total problem scores are so *high* as to raise questions about exaggeration or misunderstanding: Boys aged 5-11 >151; boys 12-18 >164; girls aged 5-11 >145; girls aged 12-18 >143.

REFERENCES

Abramowitz, M., & Stegun, I.A. (1968). *Handbook of mathematical functions*. Washington, DC: National Bureau of Standards.

Achenbach, T.M. (1966). The classification of children's psychiatric symptoms: A factor-analytic study. *Psychological Monographs, 80* (No. 615).

Achenbach, T.M. (1985). *Assessment and taxonomy of child and adolescent psychopathology*. Newbury Park, CA: Sage.

Achenbach, T.M. (1991a). *Integrative Guide for the 1991 CBCL/4-18, YSR, and TRF Profiles*. Burlington, VT: University of Vermont Department of Psychiatry.

Achenbach, T.M. (1991b). *Manual for the Child Behavior Checklist/4-18 and 1991 Profile*. Burlington, VT: University of Vermont Department of Psychiatry.

Achenbach, T.M. (1991c). *Manual for the Youth Self-Report and 1991 Profile*. Burlington, VT: University of Vermont Department of Psychiatry.

Achenbach, T.M., Bird, H.R., Canino, G.J., Phares, V., Gould, M., & Rubio-Stipec, M. (1990). Epidemiological comparisons of Puerto Rican and U.S. mainland children: Parent, teacher, and self reports. *Journal of the American Academy of Child and Adolescent Psychiatry, 29,* 84-93.

Achenbach, T.M., & Brown, J.S. (1991). *Bibliography of published studies using the Child Behavior Checklist and related materials: 1991 edition*. Burlington, VT: University of Vermont Department of Psychiatry.

Achenbach, T.M., & Edelbrock, C. (1978). The classification of child psychopathology: A review and analysis of empirical efforts. *Psychological Bulletin, 85,* 1275-1301.

Achenbach, T.M., & Edelbrock, C. (1981). Behavioral problems and competencies reported by parents of normal and disturbed children aged four to sixteen. *Monographs of the Society for Research in Child Development, 46* (Serial No. 188).

Achenbach, T.M. & Edelbrock, C. (1986). *Manual for the Teacher's Report Form and Teacher Version of the Child Behavior Profile*. Burlington, VT: University of Vermont Department of Psychiatry.

Achenbach, T.M., & Lewis, M. (1971). A proposed model for clinical research and its application to encopresis and enuresis. *Journal of the American Academy of Child Psychiatry, 10,* 535-554.

Achenbach, T.M., & McConaughy, S.H. (1987). *Empirically based assessment of child and adolescent psychopathology: Practical applications.* Newbury Park, CA: Sage.

Achenbach, T.M., Phares, V., Howell, C.T., Rauh, V.A., & Nurcombe, B. Seven-year outcome of the Vermont intervention program for low-birthweight infants. *Child Development,* 1990, *61,* 1672-1681.

Akkok, F., & Askar, P. (1989). The adaptation and standardization of the teacher version of the Child Behavior Profile: Turkish boys aged 7-12. *International Journal of Psychology, 24,* 129-136.

American Psychiatric Association (1952, 1968, 1980, 1987). *Diagnostic and statistical manual of mental disorders* (1st ed., 2nd ed., 3rd ed., 3rd ed. rev.). Washington, D.C.: Author.

Beitchman, J.H., Nair, R. Clegg, M., Ferguson, B., & Parel, P.G. (1986). Prevalence of psychiatric disorders in children with speech and language disorders. *Journal of the American Academy of Child and Adolescent Psychiatry, 25,* 528-535.

Bernstein, G.A., & Garfinkel, D.B. (1986). School phobia: The overlap of affective and anxiety disorders. *Journal of the American Academy of Child Psychiatry, 25,* 235-241.

Churchman, C.W., Ackoff, R.L., & Arnoff, E.L. (1957). *Introduction to operations research.* New York: Wiley.

Cohen, J. (1988). *Statistical power analysis for the behavioral sciences* (2nd ed.). New York: Academic Press.

Cole, D.A. (1987). Methodological contributions to clinical research: Utility of confirmatory factor analysis in test validation research. *Journal of Consulting and Clinical Psychology, 55,* 584-594.

Crocker, L., & Algina, J. (1986). *Introduction to classical and modern test theory.* New York: Holt, Rinehart, & Winston.

Cronbach, L.J. (1951). Coefficient alpha and the internal structure of tests. *Psychometrika, 16,* 297-334.

Cronbach, L.J., & Meehl, P.E. (1955). Construct validity in psychological tests. *Psychological Bulletin, 52,* 281-302.

Edelbrock, C. & Achenbach, T.M. (1984). The Teacher Version of the Child Behavior Profile: I. Boys Aged 6-11. *Journal of Consulting and Clinical Psychology, 52,* 207-217.

Edelbrock, C., Costello, A.J., Dulcan, M.K., Kalas, R., & Conover, N.C. (1985). Age differences in the reliability of the psychiatric interview of the child. *Child Development, 56,* 265-275.

Edelbrock, C., Costello, A.J., & Kessler, M.D. (1984). Empirical corroboration of attention deficit disorder. *Journal of the American Academy of Child Psychiatry, 23*, 285-290.

Education of the Handicapped Act. (1977). *Federal Register, 42*, p. 42478. Amended in *Federal Register*, (1981), *46*, p. 3866.

Evans, W.R. (1975). The Behavior Problem Checklist. Data from an inner city population. *Psychology in the Schools, 12*, 301-303.

Fleiss, J.L. (1981). *Statistical methods for rates and proportions* (2nd ed.). New York: Wiley.

Gorsuch, R.L. (1983). *Factor analysis* (2nd ed.). Hillsdale, NJ: Erlbaum.

Goyette, C.H., Conners, C.K., & Ulrich, R.F. (1978). Normative data on revised Conners Parent and Teacher Rating Scales. *Journal of Abnormal Child Psychology, 6*, 221-236.

Guilford, J.P. (1965). *Fundamental statistics in psychology and education* (4th ed.). New York: McGraw-Hill.

Harris, J.C., King, S.L., Reifler, J.P., & Rosenberg, L.A. (1984). Emotional and learning disorders in 6-12-year-old boys attending special schools. *Journal of the American Academy of Child Psychiatry, 23*, 431-437.

Hoge, R.D., & McKay, V. (1986). Criterion related validity data for the Child Behavior Checklist Teacher's Report Form. *Journal of School Psychology, 24*, 387-393.

Hollingshead, A.B. (1975). *Four factor index of social status.* Unpublished paper. New Haven, CT: Yale University, Department of Sociology.

Katz, P.A., Zigler, E., & Zalk, S.R. (1975). Children's self-image disparity: The effects of age, maladjustment and action-thought orientation. *Developmental Psychology, 11*, 546-550.

Li, X., Su, L., Townes, B.D., & Varley, C.K. (1989). Diagnosis of attention deficit disorder with hyperactivity in Chinese boys. *Journal of the American Academy of Child and Adolescent Psychiatry, 28*, 497-500.

McConaughy, S.H. (1985). Using the Child Behavior Checklist and related instruments in school-based assessment of children. *School Psychology Review, 14*, 479-494.

McConaughy, S.H., Achenbach, T.M., & Gent, C.L. (1988). Multiaxial empirically based assessment: Parent, teacher, observational, cognitive, and personality correlates of Child Behavior Profiles for 6-11-year-old boys. *Journal of Abnormal Child Psychology, 16*, 485-509.

McConaughy, S.H. & Ritter, D.R. (1986). Social competence and behavioral problems of learning disabled boys aged 6-11. *Journal of Learning Disabilities, 19*, 39-45.

McConaughy, S.H., Stanger, C., & Achenbach, T.M. (1991). Three-year course of behavioral/emotional problems in a national sample of 4- to 16-year-olds: I. Agreement among informants. *Journal of the American Academy of Child and Adolescent Psychiatry*, in press.

Milich, R., Roberts, M., Loney, J., & Caputo, J. (1980). Differentiating practice effects and statistical regression on the Conners Hyperkinesis Index. *Journal of Abnormal Child Psychology*, 8, 549-552.

Miller, L.C. (1967). Louisville Behavior Checklist for males, 6-12 years of age. *Psychological Reports*, 21, 885-896.

Miller, L.C., Hampe, E., Barrett, C.L., & Noble, H. (1972). Test-retest reliability of parent ratings of children's deviant behavior. *Psychological Reports*, 31, 249-250.

Mish, F.C. (Ed.). (1988). *Webster's ninth new collegiate dictionary.* Springfield, MA: Merriam-Webster.

Peterson, D.R. (1961). Behavior problems of middle childhood. *Journal of Consulting Psychology*, 25, 205-209.

Reed, M.L., & Edelbrock, C. (1983). Reliability and validity of the Direct Observation Form of the Child Behavior Checklist. *Journal of Abnormal Child Psychology*, 11, 521-530.

Richters, J., & Pellegrini, D. (1989). Depressed mothers' judgments about their children: An examination of the depression-distortion hypothesis. *Child Development*, 60, 1068-1075.

Sakoda, J.M., Cohen, B.H., & Beall, G. (1954). Test of significance for a series of statistical tests. *Psychological Bulletin*, 51, 172-175.

SAS Institute, (1988). *SAS/STAT User's Guide, Release 6.03 Edition.* Cary, NC: SAS Institute.

Sawyer, M.G. (1990). Childhood behavior problems: Discrepancies between reports from children, parents, and teachers. Unpublished Ph.D. dissertation. University of Adelaide, Australia.

Sawyer, M., Crettenden, A., & Toogood, I. (1986). Psychological adjustment of families of children and adolescents treated for leukemia. *American Journal of Pediatric Hematology Oncology*, 8, 200-207.

Saylor, C.F., Finch, A.J., Spirito, A., & Bennett, B. (1984). The children's depression inventory: A systematic evaluation of psychometric properties. *Journal of Consulting and Clinical Psychology*, 52, 955-967.

Snook, S.C., & Gorsuch, R.L. (1989). Component analysis versus common factor analysis: A Monte Carlo study. *Psychological Bulletin*, 106, 148-154.

Sparrow, S., Cicchetti, D.V., & Balla, D. (1984). *Vineland Social Maturity Scale-Revised.* Circle Pines, MN: American Guidance Service.

Strauss, C.C., Last, C.G., Hersen, M., & Kazdin, A.E. (1988). Association between anxiety and depression in children and adolescents with anxiety disorders. *Journal of Abnormal Child Psychology, 16,* 57-68.

Swets, J.E., & Pickett, R.M. (1982). *Evaluation of diagnostic systems: Methods from signal detection theory.* New York: Academic Press.

Treiber, F.A. & Mabe, P.A. (1987). Child and parent perceptions of children's psychopathology in psychiatric outpatient children. *Journal of Abnormal Child Psychology, 15,* 115-124.

Verhulst, F.C., & Akkerhuis, G.W. (1989). Agreement between parents' and teachers' ratings of behavioral/emotional problems of children aged 4-12. *Journal of Child Psychology and Psychiatry, 30,* 123-136.

Wechsler, D. (1989). *Wechsler Preschool and Primary Scale of Intelligence-Revised.* San Antonio: Psychological Corporation.

Weintraub, S.A. (1973). Self-control as a correlate of an internalizing-externalizing symptom dimension. *Journal of Abnormal Child Psychology, 1,* 292-307.

Weisz, J.R., Suwanlert, S., Chaiyasit, W., Weiss, B., Achenbach, T.M., & Trevathan, D. (1989). Epidemiology of behavioral and emotional problems among Thai and American children: Teacher reports for ages 6-11. *Journal of Child Psychology and Psychiatry, 30,* 471-484.

APPENDIX A
Instructions for Hand Scoring the 1991 TRF Profile

Note. Templates are available to assist in transferring data from pp. 3-4 of the TRF to the profile. The same 1991 templates are used for all four sex/age groups on the TRF. Be sure to use the profile form appropriate for the child's sex and the scale scores appropriate for the child's age. For information on ordering computer-scoring programs, write to Dr. Achenbach.

Descriptive Data Not Scored on the Profile

The following items on pp. 1-2 of the TRF are designed to provide descriptive data useful in the evaluation of individual children, but they are not scored on the profile: Items I, II, III, IV, V, VI, IX, and X.

Scoring Academic Performance and Adaptive Functioning

Item VII. For each academic subject, score the teacher's ratings as follows:

Far below grade = 1
Somewhat below grade = 2
At grade level = 3
Somewhat above grade = 4
Far above grade = 5

If a teacher checked two boxes for one subject, use the mean of the two scores assigned to these boxes.

Enter the *mean* of the teacher's ratings for all academic subjects beneath the heading *Academic Performance* on the profile. (Academic subjects include reading, writing, arithmetic, spelling, science, English, foreign language, history, social studies, etc. Do *not* count physical education, art, music, home economics, driver education, industrial arts, typing, or the like.)

Item VIII. For each of the questions 1-4, score the teacher's ratings as follows:

Much less = 1
Somewhat less = 2
Slightly less = 3
About average = 4
Slightly more = 5
Somewhat more = 6
Much more = 7

Enter the score for each rating beneath the appropriate heading on the profile.

201

Sum of Items VIII. 1-4. Sum the scores for items VIII. 1, 2, 3, and 4. Enter this sum beneath the appropriate heading on the profile. Do *not* compute this sum if any of the 4 items is missing.

Scoring the Problem Scales

Do *not* score the problem scales if data are missing for more than 8 items, not counting #56h and 113. If Items 56a-56g are left blank, you may score them 0. If a teacher circled two numbers for an item, score the item 1. Note that there are 120 items, even though the numbers range from 1-113 (Items 56a-h comprise 8 items).

ITEM SCORES—Place the 1991 TRF Page 3 template over Page 3 of the TRF. The Roman numerals beside each item number indicate the scales on which the item is scored. Enter the 0, 1, or 2 circled by the teacher on the appropriate scale of the profile. Repeat these steps using the Page 4 template on Page 4. Comments written by the teacher should be used in judging whether items deserve to be scored, with the following guidelines:

a. Only 1 item should be scored for each problem. If a teacher appears to have scored more than 1 item for the same problem, enter the teacher's rating only for the item that most precisely describes the problem.

b. For extreme behaviors (e.g., attempts suicide, physically attacks people)—if teacher noted that it happened once but circled 0 or left it blank, score 1 unless it clearly happened earlier than the 2 months specified in the rating instructions.

c. For items on which teacher noted "used to do this," score as the teacher scored it, unless it clearly occurred more than 2 months earlier.

d. When in doubt, score item the way the teacher scored it, with the following exceptions:

Item 9, obsessions—score 0 for anything that is clearly not obsessional or is more precisely covered by another item, such as *96. Seems preoccupied with sex.*

Item 28, eats or drinks things that are not food—score 0 for sweets or junk food.

Item 46, nervous movements—if "can't sit still" or anything entirely covered by item 10 is entered here, score *only* Item 10.

Item 56d, problems with eyes—score 0 for "wears glasses," "nearsighted," and other visual problems having an organic basis.

Item 66, compulsions—score 0 for noncompulsive behavior; e.g., "keeps hitting others."

Item 84, strange behavior, & 85, strange ideas—if what the teacher described is specifically covered by another item, score the more specific item instead, such as *34. Feels others are out to get him/her.*

Item 105, alcohol or drugs—score 0 for tobacco and for drugs used medicinally.

Item 113, additional problems—score only if *not* specifically covered by another item; if teacher entered more than 1 item here, count only the highest rating toward the total behavior problem score; e.g., if any problem listed in 113 was rated 2, add 2 to total score; if the highest rating for any problem listed in 113 was 1, add 1 to total score.

SYNDROME SCALE SCORES—To obtain the total raw score for each syndrome scale, sum the 0s, 1s, and 2s you have entered for each scale. Because the items listed under *Other Problems* do not form a scale, a total score is *not* computed for them.

GRAPHIC DISPLAY AND T SCORES—To complete the graphic display for the adaptive and syndrome scales, make an X on the number above each scale that equals the total score obtained for that scale. *Be sure to mark the number in the column appropriate for the pupil's age.* Then draw a line to connect the Xs. Percentiles based on nonreferred pupils can be read from the left side of the graphic display. *T* scores can be read from the right side.

INTERNALIZING AND EXTERNALIZING—A box at the bottom of the problem profile outlines the computation of Internalizing and Externalizing scores as follows: *Internalizing* = the sum of raw scores for syndrome Scales I + II + III, minus the score for Item 103 to avoid counting Item 103 twice, because it is on both Scale I and III. *Externalizing* = the sum of raw scores for syndrome Scales VII + VIII. A *T* score for each Internalizing and Externalizing raw score is listed in the box to the right of the profile. *Be sure to look at the raw score column for the age of the pupil being scored.*

TOTAL PROBLEM SCORE—To compute the total problem score, sum the 1s and 2s on the TRF and enter the sum in the box to the far right of the profile. If the teacher entered a problem for Item 56h or 113 that is not covered by another item, include the score for 56h or 113. If more than one problem has been entered for Item 113, count only the one having the highest score. The total problem score can be cross-checked by subtracting the number of items scored as present from the sum of 1s and 2s. The difference should equal the number of 2s. (The number and sum of items can *not* be computed by adding scale totals, because some items appear on more than one scale.) A *T* score for each total problem score is listed in the box to the right of the profile. *Be sure to look at the total score column for the age of the pupil being scored.*

APPENDIX B
TRF Scale Scores for Matched Referred and Nonreferred Boys 5-11

Scale	T Score Referred Mean	SD	T Score Nonreferred Mean	SD	Raw Score Referred Mean	SD	Raw Score Nonreferred Mean	SD	SE of Mean[a] Ref	Nonref	SE of Meas[b] Ref	Nonref	Cronbach's alpha
Academic Performance	40.4	7.5	50.2	8.5	2.1	.9	3.2	.8	.0	.0	.2	.2	N/A
Working Hard	43.5	8.1	50.2	8.5	2.8	1.6	4.1	1.6	.1	.1	.4	.4	N/A
Behaving Appropriately	41.7	7.8	50.4	8.8	2.6	1.6	4.3	1.7	.1	.1	.7	.7	N/A
Learning	42.1	7.4	50.2	8.3	2.9	1.5	4.5	1.4	.1	.1	.4	.4	N/A
Happy	42.7	6.8	50.5	7.8	3.1	1.4	4.6	1.3	.1	.1	.7	.7	N/A
Total Adaptive	40.5	7.2	49.9	8.7	11.5	5.0	17.5	5.1	.3	.3	1.3	1.3	N/A
Withdrawn	60.2	9.7	54.2	6.3	4.2	3.9	1.8	2.5	.2	.1	1.0	.7	.83
Somatic Complaints	55.2	7.6	52.9	6.2	.9	1.7	.5	1.4	.1	.1	.7	.6	.72
Anxious/Depressed	59.3	9.5	54.1	5.9	6.6	6.4	3.2	3.7	.3	.2	2.1	1.2	.88
Social Problems	63.0	9.0	54.1	6.1	5.9	4.6	1.8	2.7	.3	.1	1.3	.8	.85
Thought Problems	58.2	10.2	52.4	5.3	1.6	2.4	.4	.8	.1	.0	1.0	.3	.72
Attention Problems	62.3	10.3	54.1	6.2	18.8	9.8	8.7	8.5	.5	.5	2.2	1.9	.94
Delinquent Behavior	59.7	8.2	54.0	5.7	3.1	2.8	1.3	1.8	.2	.1	.8	.5	.70
Aggressive Behavior	61.7	10.9	54.0	6.1	15.8	12.6	6.0	8.2	.7	.4	5.0	3.2	.96
Internalizing	58.3	12.2	50.2	9.7	11.1	9.5	5.3	5.6	.5	.3	2.7	1.6	.90
Externalizing	60.3	10.9	50.3	9.4	19.0	14.7	7.2	9.6	.8	.5	5.5	3.6	.96
Total Problems	62.3	10.3	50.1	9.8	56.5	32.1	23.5	21.9	1.8	1.2	8.9	6.1	.97

Note. N = 334 each in demographically matched referred and nonreferred samples described in Chapter 6. [a]Standard error of mean raw scores. [b]Standard error of measurement = SD√1-reliability (Guilford, 1965) computed from reliability of raw scores shown in Table 5-1.

APPENDIX B (continued)
TRF Scale Scores for Matched Referred and Nonreferred Boys 12-18

Scale	T Score Referred Mean	SD	T Score Nonreferred Mean	SD	Raw Score Referred Mean	SD	Raw Score Nonreferred Mean	SD	SE of Mean[a] Ref	Nonref	SE of Meas[b] Ref	Nonref	Cronbach's alpha
Academic Performance	41.9	7.1	49.9	8.9	2.0	.9	3.0	1.0	.1	.1	.2	.2	N/A
Working Hard	44.2	8.0	49.9	8.7	2.8	1.7	4.0	1.8	.1	.1	.4	.5	N/A
Behaving Appropriately	41.4	7.8	50.0	8.6	2.8	.6	4.5	1.6	.1	.1	.7	.7	N/A
Learning	42.5	6.9	49.7	8.4	2.7	1.5	4.3	.7	.1	.1	.4	.5	N/A
Happy	41.9	7.4	49.7	8.4	3.0	1.6	4.5	1.5	.1	.1	.8	.8	N/A
Total Adaptive	41.6	7.2	50.0	8.6	11.3	5.3	17.3	5.9	.3	.4	1.4	1.5	N/A
Withdrawn	59.3	8.1	54.1	6.5	4.6	3.8	2.1	3.1	.2	.2	1.0	.8	.84
Somatic Complaints	54.7	7.2	53.0	6.4	.9	1.7	.6	1.6	.1	.1	.7	.7	.74
Anxious/Depressed	61.1	8.8	54.1	6.0	7.6	6.4	2.8	4.0	.4	.2	2.1	1.3	.89
Social Problems	61.1	7.2	54.4	6.2	5.5	4.3	2.1	3.2	.3	.2	1.3	.9	.84
Thought Problems	59.4	10.2	52.5	5.5	1.8	2.4	.4	1.0	.2	.1	1.0	.4	.70
Attention Problems	59.4	7.7	54.3	6.6	16.9	8.8	9.0	9.1	.5	.6	1.9	2.0	.93
Delinquent Behavior	61.0	9.1	54.1	6.6	4.5	3.9	1.6	2.7	.2	.2	1.1	.8	.82
Aggressive Behavior	63.0	11.3	54.3	6.7	16.4	13.1	5.6	8.2	.8	.5	5.2	3.2	.96
Internalizing	59.6	8.9	50.7	9.4	12.4	9.0	5.3	6.8	.6	.4	2.6	1.9	.90
Externalizing	61.6	10.8	50.9	9.4	20.9	16.2	7.2	10.3	1.0	.6	6.0	3.8	.96
Total Problems	62.2	9.1	50.7	10.0	57.8	32.3	24.3	26.3	2.0	1.6	9.0	7.3	.97

Note. N = 259 each in demographically matched referred and nonreferred samples described in Chapter 6. [a]Standard error of mean raw scores. [b]Standard error of measurement = SD√1-reliability (Guilford, 1965) computed from reliability of raw scores shown in Table 5-1.

APPENDIX B (continued)
TRF Scale Scores for Matched Referred and Nonreferred Girls 5-11

Scale	T Score Referred Mean	SD	Nonreferred Mean	SD	Raw Score Referred Mean	SD	Nonreferred Mean	SD	SE of Mean[a] Ref	Nonref	SE of Meas[b] Ref	Nonref	Cronbach's alpha
Academic Performance	39.9	7.4	49.9	8.7	2.2	.9	3.3	.8	.0	.0	.3	.2	N/A
Working Hard	42.8	7.7	50.4	8.8	3.2	1.6	4.7	1.6	.1	.1	.4	.4	N/A
Behaving Appropriately	42.3	8.2	50.1	8.5	3.4	1.8	5.1	1.5	.1	.1	.7	.6	N/A
Learning	41.1	7.7	50.0	8.7	3.1	1.5	4.8	1.4	.1	.1	.6	.5	N/A
Happy	42.5	6.9	50.6	8.2	3.5	1.5	5.0	1.4	.1	.1	.5	.5	N/A
Total Adaptive	40.4	7.1	50.0	8.7	13.2	5.3	19.6	5.0	.3	.3	1.3	1.2	N/A
Withdrawn	58.8	9.5	54.0	6.3	3.8	3.7	1.8	2.6	.2	.1	.8	.6	.83
Somatic Complaints	54.9	7.5	52.9	5.9	1.2	2.1	.7	1.6	.1	.1	.3	.2	.76
Anxious/Depressed	59.0	8.8	54.1	6.1	6.5	6.2	3.1	4.0	.3	.2	2.5	1.6	.89
Social Problems	61.7	9.8	53.9	5.9	5.3	5.1	1.6	2.7	.3	.1	.6	.3	.87
Thought Problems	56.7	8.9	52.2	5.2	1.1	1.8	.3	.8	.1	.0	1.4	.6	.63
Attention Problems	63.5	11.0	54.1	6.3	15.3	10.1	5.5	6.9	.5	.4	1.3	.9	.95
Delinquent Behavior	58.8	9.3	53.7	6.0	2.1	2.6	.8	1.4	.1	.1	.9	.5	.69
Aggressive Behavior	61.6	11.2	54.0	5.9	11.1	11.9	3.5	5.8	.6	.3	1.9	1.0	.96
Internalizing	57.4	10.5	50.3	9.5	10.9	9.4	5.5	6.4	.5	.3	3.3	2.3	.91
Externalizing	59.8	11.9	50.7	8.8	13.2	13.8	4.2	6.8	.7	.4	2.5	1.2	.95
Total Problems	61.6	10.7	50.2	9.8	45.3	32.0	17.2	19.0	1.6	1.0	3.4	2.0	.97

Note. $N = 379$ each in demographically matched referred and nonreferred samples described in Chapter 6. [a]Standard error of mean raw scores. [b]Standard error of measurement = $SD\sqrt{1\text{-reliability}}$ (Guilford, 1965) computed from reliability of raw scores shown in Table 5-1.

APPENDIX B (continued)
TRF Scale Scores for Matched Referred and Nonreferred Girls 12-18

Scale	T Score Referred Mean	SD	T Score Nonreferred Mean	SD	Raw Score Referred Mean	SD	Raw Score Nonreferred Mean	SD	SE of Mean[a] Ref	Nonref	SE of Meas[b] Ref	Nonref	Cronbach's alpha
Academic Performance	39.7	7.0	51.1	9.4	2.1	0.9	3.4	1.0	0.1	0.1	0.3	0.3	N/A
Working Hard	41.7	7.2	50.1	8.2	3.0	1.7	4.9	1.6	0.1	0.1	0.4	0.4	N/A
Behaving Appropriately	41.8	7.0	50.3	7.8	3.3	1.8	5.3	1.6	0.1	0.1	0.7	0.6	N/A
Learning	40.6	6.0	50.4	8.2	2.9	1.5	5.0	1.5	0.1	0.1	0.6	0.5	N/A
Happy	41.4	6.2	50.8	8.2	2.9	1.5	4.9	1.5	0.1	0.1	0.5	0.5	N/A
Total Adaptive	39.5	6.0	50.1	8.5	12.0	5.5	20.1	5.3	0.3	0.3	1.3	1.3	N/A
Withdrawn	60.7	9.4	53.8	6.1	4.6	3.9	1.7	2.6	0.2	0.1	0.9	0.6	0.84
Somatic Complaints	56.6	9.5	52.0	4.9	1.4	2.7	0.3	1.0	0.2	0.1	0.4	0.1	0.84
Anxious/Depressed	61.1	8.6	53.9	5.8	7.9	6.2	2.9	3.9	0.4	0.2	2.6	1.6	0.89
Social Problems	63.3	9.1	54.0	6.0	5.5	4.9	1.4	2.5	0.3	0.1	0.5	0.3	0.87
Thought Problems	56.9	9.0	52.1	5.1	1.2	1.9	0.3	0.8	0.1	0.0	1.4	0.6	0.65
Attention Problems	63.3	9.3	53.9	6.0	14.4	8.9	4.7	6.3	0.5	0.4	1.2	0.8	0.94
Delinquent Behavior	62.3	10.7	53.6	5.5	3.8	3.9	0.9	1.6	0.2	0.1	1.3	0.5	0.81
Aggressive Behavior	63.1	11.2	54.3	6.6	12.8	12.6	3.3	6.6	0.7	0.4	2.1	1.1	0.97
Internalizing	60.6	10.0	50.2	9.1	13.1	9.8	4.8	6.1	0.6	0.3	3.5	2.2	0.92
Externalizing	62.2	11.3	50.7	9.0	16.7	15.6	4.3	7.8	0.9	0.4	2.8	1.4	0.96
Total Problems	64.3	9.9	50.3	9.8	51.0	33.2	15.4	19.5	1.9	1.1	3.5	2.0	0.98

Note. N = 303 each in demographically matched referred and nonreferred samples described in Chapter 6.
[a]Standard error of mean raw scores. [b]Standard error of measurement = $SD\sqrt{1\text{-reliability}}$ (Guilford, 1965) computed from reliability of raw scores shown in Table 5-1.

APPENDIX C

Pearson Corrlations among TRF *T* Scores for Boys aged 5-11
Referred Sample above Diagonal, Nonreferred Sample below Diagonal

	Acad Perf	Work Hard	Beh App	Lrn	Hap	Tot Adpt	With-drn	Som	Anx/ Dep	Soc Prob	Tht Prob	Att	Del	Agg	Int	Ext	Tot Prob
Academic Perform		.39	.19	.60	.11	.39	-.13	-.17	-.01	-.20	-.15	-.35	-.19	-.10	-.09	-.15	-.28
Working Hard	.58		.62	.72	.48	.85	-.16	-.13	.07	-.29	-.24	-.53	-.34	-.30	-.04	-.37	-.43
Behaves Approp.	.45	.67		.49	.56	.82	-.10	-.09	-.10	-.40	-.34	-.45	-.47	-.54	-.10	-.61	-.55
Learning	.82	.74	.60		.42	.80	-.19	-.16	-.03	-.26	-.19	-.45	-.27	-.20	-.11	-.27	-.38
Happy	.50	.59	.54	.60		.70	-.40	-.22	-.37	-.43	-.31	-.35	-.35	-.36	-.44	-.42	-.51
Total Adaptive	.68	.89	.84	.85	.78		-.23	-.17	-.10	-.39	-.32	-.51	-.43	-.41	-.17	-.50	-.55
Withdrawn	-.34	-.41	-.18	-.38	-.43	-.40		.36	.35	.47	.39	.45	.22	.12	.81	.15	.52
Somatic Comp.	-.20	-.19	-.13	-.19	-.19	-.21	.27		.35	.36	.30	.33	.22	.10	.52	.15	.40
Anx/Depressed	-.12	-.11	-.10	-.12	-.29	-.17	.45	.19		.67	.42	.34	.27	.34	.89	.34	.63
Social Problems	-.39	-.47	-.47	-.43	-.43	-.52	.45	.29	.54		.55	.63	.45	.54	.66	.58	.82
Thought Problems	-.20	-.31	-.33	-.26	-.22	-.35	.34	.31	.30	.45		.55	.33	.39	.46	.40	.62
Attention Prob.	-.48	-.67	-.60	-.58	-.39	-.68	.43	.29	.27	.61	.50		.40	.43	.44	.48	.75
Delinquent	-.27	-.42	-.55	-.37	-.35	-.51	.17	.20	.17	.42	.33	.49		.70	.30	.79	.68
Aggressive	-.29	-.44	-.65	-.37	-.32	-.55	.15	.20	.23	.56	.45	.65	.75		.29	.94	.77
Internalizing	-.26	-.28	-.17	-.28	-.38	-.32	.71	.44	.80	.56	.40	.42	.25	.27		.32	.68
Externalizing	-.30	-.50	-.68	-.41	-.32	-.58	.15	.22	.24	.53	.39	.60	.78	.89	.30		.83
Total Problems	-.45	-.64	-.65	-.57	-.48	-.71	.51	.39	.50	.70	.52	.77	.66	.75	.68	.81	

Note. Samples are demographically matched referred and nonreferred pupils. *N* = 334 in each sample for problem scales, *rs* >.11 were significant at *p* <.05.

APPENDIX C (continued)

Pearson Corrlations among TRF *T* Scores for Boys aged 12-18
Referred Sample above Diagonal, Nonreferred Sample below Diagonal

	Perf	Hard	App	Lrn	Hap	Tot Adpt	With-drn	Som	Anx/Dep	Soc Prob	Tht Prob	Att	Del	Agg	Int	Ext	Tot Prob
Academic Perform		.44	.36	.60	.30	.51	-.15	-.16	-.16	-.24	-.19	-.38	-.26	-.29	-.23	-.34	-.41
Working Hard	.76		.68	.73	.56	.88	-.15	-.21	.03	-.14	-.14	-.51	-.41	-.31	-.07	-.37	-.41
Behaving Approp.	.59	.73		.56	.54	.83	-.12	-.20	-.11	-.38	-.29	-.47	-.45	-.47	-.16	-.54	-.55
Learning	.79	.87	.67		.47	.82	-.14	-.19	-.07	-.26	-.18	-.51	-.36	-.28	-.15	-.34	-.44
Happy	.64	.71	.61	.75		.75	-.33	-.21	-.29	-.30	-.28	-.33	-.37	-.28	-.38	-.30	-.44
Total Adaptive	.78	.94	.85	.92	.84		-.22	-.23	-.14	-.33	-.28	-.52	-.46	-.39	-.23	-.45	-.55
Withdrawn	-.41	-.42	-.22	-.39	-.49	-.43		.30	.49	.35	.37	.33	.15	.05	.74	.06	.41
Somatic Comp.	-.33	-.35	-.27	-.33	-.37	-.36	.38		.24	.26	.30	.40	.26	.24	.43	.25	.44
Anx/Depressed	-.22	-.27	-.23	-.22	-.33	-.30	.62	.41		.72	.51	.34	.23	.31	.89	.31	.61
Social Problems	-.38	-.48	-.47	-.38	-.47	-.51	.57	.48	.73		.54	.52	.32	.50	.67	.50	.74
Thought Problems	-.34	-.37	-.39	-.35	-.35	-.41	.43	.30	.43	.54		.52	.39	.36	.52	.41	.63
Attention Probs.	-.60	-.66	-.59	-.61	-.54	-.68	.53	.54	.54	.74	.58		.50	.56	.43	.58	.77
Delinquent	-.46	-.48	-.48	-.46	-.43	-.51	.40	.41	.41	.51	.57	.63		.71	.27	.81	.71
Aggressive	-.38	-.46	-.59	-.40	-.37	-.51	.26	.30	.42	.61	.43	.71	.76		.30	.95	.81
Internalizing	-.37	-.39	-.31	-.36	-.44	-.42	.77	.56	.84	.70	.55	.61	.47	.41		.31	.68
Externalizing	-.42	-.50	-.63	-.45	-.38	-.55	.30	.34	.46	.61	.55	.68	.79	.90	.48		.84
Total Problems	-.59	-.65	-.64	-.60	-.56	-.69	.60	.52	.67	.78	.58	.82	.70	.76	.78	.85	

Note. Samples are demographically matched referred and nonreferred pupils. *N* = 259 in each sample for problem scales, *r*s >.12 were significant at *p* <.05.

APPENDIX C (continued)
Pearson Corrlations among TRF T Scores for Girls aged 5-11
Referred Sample above Diagonal, Nonreferred Sample below Diagonal

	Acad Perf	Work Hard	Beh App	Lrn	Tot Hap	Adpt	With-drn	Som	Anx/Dep	Soc Prob	Tht Prob	Att	Del	Agg	Int	Ext	Tot Prob
Academic Perform		.40	.20	.62	.15	.42	-.23	-.09	-.20	-.32	-.10	-.46	-.18	-.17	-.26	-.19	-.39
Working Hard	.61		.59	.70	.46	.82	-.30	-.14	-.19	-.42	-.24	-.60	-.36	-.38	-.25	-.41	-.52
Behaving Approp.	.34	.65		.53	.59	.81	-.16	-.08	-.23	-.47	-.34	-.47	-.40	-.55	-.21	-.59	-.52
Learning	.73	.79	.56		.50	.82	-.28	-.12	-.23	-.42	-.23	-.56	-.25	-.28	-.28	-.30	-.48
Happy	.44	.57	.57	.62		.74	-.40	-.18	-.35	-.37	-.29	-.33	-.29	-.30	-.39	-.34	-.42
Total Adaptive	.62	.89	.82	.87	.80		-.32	-.14	-.28	-.48	-.31	-.55	-.36	-.41	-.31	-.47	-.56
Withdrawn	-.29	-.32	-.17	-.32	-.41	-.36		.28	.62	.51	.46	.47	.26	.14	.77	.20	.55
Somatic Comp.	-.07	-.19	-.21	-.16	-.26	-.23	.35		.35	.39	.23	.28	.19	.14	.52	.20	.38
Anx/Depressed	-.07	-.06	-.10	-.10	-.29	-.15	.52	.39		.73	.52	.45	.32	.38	.88	.40	.67
Social Problems	-.26	-.37	-.42	-.36	-.45	-.47	.50	.40	.64		.57	.68	.53	.63	.71	.65	.84
Thought Problems	-.22	-.25	-.28	-.23	-.22	-.29	.28	.21	.31	.45		.50	.41	.49	.53	.49	.63
Attention Probs.	-.51	-.61	-.45	-.58	-.42	-.61	.54	.33	.35	.62	.43		.47	.55	.52	.58	.81
Delinquent	-.24	-.34	-.41	-.31	-.31	-.39	.29	.32	.26	.42	.39	.49		.73	.36	.80	.69
Aggressive	-.21	-.41	-.59	-.37	-.35	-.50	.22	.34	.40	.66	.47	.59	.66		.35	.96	.78
Internalizing	-.18	-.17	-.15	-.21	-.37	-.25	.72	.54	.82	.61	.34	.45	.34	.38		.40	.75
Externalizing	-.25	-.45	-.60	-.40	-.38	-.53	.29	.35	.40	.65	.45	.61	.75	.93	.43		.82
Total Problems	-.39	-.51	-.51	-.49	-.48	-.58	.59	.46	.61	.73	.48	.76	.62	.74	.76	.81	

Note. Samples are demographically matched referred and nonreferred pupils. $N = 379$ in each sample for problem scales, rs $>.10$ were significant at $p <.05$.

APPENDIX C (continued)

Pearson Corrlations among TRF T Scores for Girls aged 12-18

Referred Sample above Diagonal, Nonreferred Sample below Diagonal

	Acad Perf	Work Hard	Beh App	Lrn	Hap	Tot Adpt	With-drn	Som	Anx/Dep	Soc Prob	Tht Prob	Att	Del	Agg	Int	Ext	Tot Prob
Academic Perform		.49	.27	.67	.23	.48	-.20	-.07	-.14	-.21	-.07	-.40	-.21	-.16	-.20	-.21	-.35
Working Hard	.70		.64	.73	.49	.86	-.25	-.14	-.09	-.29	-.21	-.54	-.44	-.37	-.20	-.45	-.51
Behaving Approp.	.51	.67		.58	.47	.81	-.06	-.15	-.16	-.39	-.33	-.51	-.53	-.62	-.17	-.67	-.60
Learning	.80	.82	.66		.45	.81	-.22	-.10	-.15	-.30	-.22	-.56	-.38	-.34	-.21	-.40	-.50
Happy	.45	.57	.63	.60		.70	-.50	-.25	-.43	-.49	-.39	-.45	-.45	-.38	-.52	-.45	-.59
Total Adaptive	.70	.88	.85	.89	.82		-.29	-.17	-.24	-.43	-.32	-.59	-.51	-.48	-.32	-.57	-.64
Withdrawn	-.37	-.28	-.24	-.28	-.47	-.38		.27	.56	.45	.30	.43	.21	.09	.74	.14	.49
Somatic Comp.	-.26	-.19	-.19	-.18	-.27	-.25	.50		.40	.40	.37	.30	.31	.28	.57	.31	.45
Anx/Depressed	-.22	-.14	-.25	-.16	-.41	-.29	.64	.46		.72	.48	.50	.25	.39	.90	.39	.68
Social Problems	-.39	-.37	-.47	-.38	-.51	-.52	.59	.47	.79		.50	.63	.39	.56	.70	.56	.78
Thought Problems	-.26	-.30	-.37	-.28	-.31	-.38	.42	.42	.49	.58		.54	.37	.49	.48	.47	.61
Attention Prob.	-.60	-.64	-.56	-.59	-.46	-.66	.49	.34	.48	.67	.57		.43	.61	.54	.59	.82
Delinquent	-.35	-.48	-.45	-.36	-.38	-.48	.36	.34	.33	.49	.50	.58		.70	.31	.82	.68
Aggressive	-.30	-.39	-.57	-.35	-.41	-.50	.29	.35	.50	.65	.56	.63	.62		.35	.95	.81
Internalizing	-.34	-.26	-.27	-.28	-.47	-.38	.77	.54	.85	.71	.46	.51	.37	.40		.37	.73
Externalizing	-.37	-.47	-.60	-.40	-.46	-.55	.32	.37	.49	.65	.52	.65	.76	.91	.45		.83
Total Problems	-.52	-.55	-.58	-.52	-.58	-.65	.61	.49	.71	.78	.58	.78	.65	.75	.79	.82	

Note. Samples are demographically matched referred and nonreferred pupils. $N = 303$ in each sample for problem scales, $rs > .11$ were significant at $p < .05$.

INDEX

Abramowitz, M., 19, 39, 196
Academic Performance, 4, 14-21, 81-85, 90-94, 181, 201
Achenbach, T.M., 1, 3, 4, 10, 16, 23, 49, 54, 69, 133, 150, 183, 196-200
Achievement, 146, 152, 170, 173
Ackoff, R.L., 175, 197
Adaptive functioning, 4, 14-22, 90-94
Administration of the TRF, 11, 147, 170, 172, 175, 185
Age differences, 102
Aggressive Behavior, 28, 49, 61, 62, 69, 156
Akkerhuis, G.W., 178, 200
Akkok, F., 178, 197
Algina, J., 19, 197
American Association on Mental Deficiency's Adaptive Behavior Scales, 143
American Psychiatric Association, 170, 197
Anxiety, 128
Anxious/Depressed, 29, 49, 127
Arnoff, E.L., 175, 197
Askar, P., 178, 197
Attention Problems, 38, 51, 144, 156
Balla, D., 143, 200
Barrett, C.L., 59, 199
Beall, G., 59, 199
Beitchman, J.H., 178, 197
Bennett, B., 199
Bernstein, G.A., 128, 197
Bird, H.R., 196
Borderline clinical range, 45-47, 52, 79
Brown, J.S., 69, 133, 164, 196
Canino, G.J., 196
Caputo, J., 59, 199
Chaiyasit, W., 200
Child abuse, 176
Child Behavior Checklist for Ages 4-18 (CBCL/4-18), 10, 147-153

Churchman, C.W., 175, 197
Cicchetti, D.V., 143, 200
Clegg, M., 178, 197
Cognitive, 69, 141-143, 146, 170-173
Cohen, B.H., 59, 199
Cohen J., 73, 91, 102, 123, 197
Cole, D.A., 128, 197
Common items, 30
Computer-scored profile, 16, 52, 167, 192
Conduct Problems, 69
Confidentiality, 12
Conners, C.K., 69, 198, 199
Connors' Revised Teacher Rating Scale, 69-70
Conover, N.C., 59, 197
Construct validity, 68-71
Content validity, 66
Core syndromes, 30, 31, 127
Costello, A.J., 59, 70, 197, 198
Crettenden, A., 178, 199
Criterion-related validity, 71-86
Crocker, L., 19, 197
Cronbach, L.J., 58, 68, 197
Cronbach's alpha, 58, 204-207
Cross-cultural research, 177-178
Cross-informant syndromes, 30, 32-34, 68, 127
Cross-informant correlations, 181-182
Cutpoints, 46-47, 79-83
Delinquent Behavior, 32, 49, 193
Demographic differences, 75, 92, 102
Depressed mothers, 173-174
Depression, 128
Diagnostic and Statistical Manual (DSM), 127, 170
Direct Observation Form (DOF), 5, 147-153, 160
Dulcan, M.K., 59, 197
Edelbrock, C., 1, 16, 23, 26, 49, 59, 67, 70-72, 196-199